But feeling much
Better Now!

CHARLES DICKENS

CHARLES
DICKENS

Other titles in the
People Who Made History series:

CHARLES DICKENS

Harold Maltz and Miriam Maltz, *Book Editors*

Daniel Leone, *President*
Bonnie Szumski, *Publisher*
Scott Barbour, *Managing Editor*
David M. Haugen, *Series Editor*

GREENHAVEN
PRESS ®

THOMSON
————✦————
GALE

San Diego • Detroit • New York • San Francisco • Cleveland
New Haven, Conn. • Waterville, Maine • London • Munich

LIBRARY OF CONGRESS CATALOGING-IN-PUBLICATION DATA

Charles Dickens / Harold Maltz, book editor, Miriam Maltz, book editor.
   p. cm. — (People who made history)
  Includes bibliographical references and index.
  ISBN 0-7377-1601-0 (lib. bdg. : alk. paper) —
  ISBN 0-7377-1602-9 (pbk. : alk. paper)
   1. Dickens, Charles, 1812–1870. 2. Novelists, English—19th century—Biography.
I. Maltz, Harold. II. Maltz, Miriam. II. Series.
PR4581 .C47 2003
823'.8—dc21
                        2002042612

Contents

Chapter 5: Dickens's Literary Reputation

FOREWORD

In the vast and colorful pageant of human history, a handful of individuals stand out. They are the men and women who have come variously to be called "great," "leading," "brilliant," "pivotal," or "infamous" because they and their deeds forever changed their own society or the world as a whole. Some were political or military leaders—kings, queens, presidents, generals, and the like—whose policies, conquests, or innovations reshaped the maps and futures of countries and entire continents. Among those falling into this category were the formidable Roman statesman/general Julius Caesar, who extended Rome's power into Gaul (what is now France); Caesar's lover and ally, the notorious Egyptian queen Cleopatra, who challenged the strongest male rulers of her day; and England's stalwart Queen Elizabeth I, whose defeat of the mighty Spanish Armada saved England from subjugation.

Some of history's other movers and shakers were scientists or other thinkers whose ideas and discoveries altered the way people conduct their everyday lives or view themselves and their place in nature. The electric light and other remarkable inventions of Thomas Edison, for example, revolutionized almost every aspect of home-life and the workplace; and the theories of naturalist Charles Darwin lit the way for biologists and other scientists in their ongoing efforts to understand the origins of living things, including human beings.

Still other people who made history were religious leaders and social reformers. The struggles of the Arabic prophet Muhammad more than a thousand years ago led to the establishment of one of the world's great religions—Islam; and the efforts and personal sacrifices of an American reverend named Martin Luther King Jr. brought about major improvements in race relations and the justice system in the United States.

Each anthology in the People Who Made History series begins with an introductory essay that provides a general overview of the individual's life, times, and contributions. The group of essays that follow are chosen for their accessibility to a young adult audience and carefully edited in consideration of the reading and comprehension levels of that audience. Some of the essays are by noted historians, professors, and other experts. Others are excerpts from contemporary writings by or about the pivotal individual in question. To aid the reader in choosing the material of immediate interest or need, an annotated table of contents summarizes the article's main themes and insights.

Each volume also contains extensive research tools, including a collection of excerpts from primary source documents pertaining to the individual under discussion. The volumes are rounded out with an extensive bibliography and a comprehensive index.

Plutarch, the renowned first-century Greek biographer and moralist, crystallized the idea behind Greenhaven's People Who Made History when he said, "To be ignorant of the lives of the most celebrated men of past ages is to continue in a state of childhood all our days." Indeed, since it is people who make history, every modern nation, organization, institution, invention, artifact, and idea is the result of the diligent efforts of one or more individuals, living or dead; and it is therefore impossible to understand how the world we live in came to be without examining the contributions of these individuals.

INTRODUCTION: THE AUTHOR AND THE REFORMER

Charles Dickens had millions of devoted readers, both in England and abroad, during his lifetime. According to a friend and contemporary, biographer John Forster, he was undoubtedly "the most popular novelist of the century."[1] Forster's assessment is confirmed by twentieth-century scholars. T.W. Heyck, a commentator on the Victorian era, maintains that "certainly he was the most widely read of the Victorian authors."[2] Philip Collins, the author of several books on Dickens, calls him "a voice of his age."[3] And Gordon Marsden, an editor of Victorian studies, notes Dickens's widespread appeal: "He touched all classes of Victorian society from the Queen to the road sweeper."[4] Indeed, no English writer since William Shakespeare has garnered more popular acclaim.

ACCOUNTING FOR DICKENS'S POPULARITY

What did Dickens do to merit such widespread praise? Most scholars and biographers agree that the basis of his fame was twofold: He was the great Victorian writer, the author of extraordinarily popular and influential essays and novels and he was also the great reformer, demanding an end to corruption and advocating radical changes in education, the administration of the law, and the running of prisons.

The popularity of his works in turn depended on a number of factors. Dickens lived at a time when lower- and middle-class readership had expanded enormously. As education became more easily available, literacy became more widespread. As Heyck indicates, the size of the reading public had vastly increased from an estimated 80,000 during the 1790s to somewhere between 2 and 5 million readers in England and Wales by 1830.[5]

The introduction into England of a method of publication that had been used in France—namely, the serialization of novels in monthly (or weekly) installments—reduced the price of books, making them more affordable. In 1836 a full-length novel cost thirty-one shillings, whereas a monthly installment of thirty-two pages could be purchased for only one shilling. Dickens was the first English novelist to utilize this innovation in publishing. Although not all writers could cope with the stress of serial publication, with its strict deadlines, Dickens flourished. His novels were usually divided into twenty episodes and were published in nineteen monthly installments (with the final installment a double episode). In addition to serial publication, the establishment of lending libraries made books more readily available. People could thus obtain books more easily and more cheaply than ever before.

The advent of widespread reading helped create an atmosphere of intellectual stimulus, one that encouraged writers to produce more books—fiction, essays, histories, biographies, political treatises, and scientific works—for an increasingly educated and prosperous readership. Many thousands of novels were published during the Victorian era because the reading public preferred novels to all other forms of literature. Marsden attempts to describe the enormous popularity of Dickens's serialized novels: "The serialized publication of many of his novels attracted the same sort of public fascination and interest in his characters as many of today's TV 'soap operas.'"[6]

The success of Dickens's agitation for reform likewise depended on a number of factors. The same circumstances that helped Dickens's works become unprecedently popular also helped his political efforts. Dickens did not stand outside Britain's Parliament brandishing a banner or sign, nor did he participate in street demonstrations. Instead, he wrote about the suffering, poverty, exploitation, and injustice that afflicted the lower classes. He was not embarrassed to abandon all restraint in his writing, to employ every device of melodrama in order to arouse sympathy and tears and to awaken the consciences of his readers in the hope that they would be induced to take political action leading ultimately to reform. Commenting on this strategy, Walter E. Houghton, the eminent social historian writes:

> Dickens was recognized as a major prophet of sympathetic feeling and benevolent action. . . . This ethical message is related, in a significant way, to the negative character of Dick-

ens's social criticism. He attacked various abuses—prisons, boarding schools, the Court of Chancery—but he had no positive theory of reform. . . . The only remedy he could think of was to melt the cold indifference of the fashionable world and the hard, two-fisted insensitivity of the Gradgrinds [in *Hard Times*] by the warm breath of pity and kindness; and by that inspiration stimulate an active life of private charity.[7]

Dickens, then, was no political theorist. Instead, he believed in what is termed *amelioration of suffering*—that is, in improving the lot of the unfortunate, not through bureaucratic organizations but rather through the kind deeds and charity of individuals, actions that would lead eventually to parliamentary reform. Critics could argue that amelioration focused on the symptoms rather than the root causes. Nevertheless, Dickens gave a voice to the voiceless, to the millions of poor and oppressed who had neither vote nor power, and for that they—and those who sought justice—loved him. Dickens's compassion for society's victims continued to manifest itself throughout his adult life, as did his continued efforts, through his writings, to make England a kinder and more humane place. Robert Alan Donovan sums up the ongoing concerns of Dickens's novels: "If anything can supply an intelligible principle of Dickens's development as a novelist, it is the constant strengthening and focusing of his protest against social injustice."[8]

THE BLACKING FACTORY

From his birth in Portsmouth, England, on February 7, 1812, until the age of twelve, Dickens passed through the typical stages of English childhood. At the time of his birth, Dickens's father was a naval clerk and the family was solidly middle class, but as their fortunes declined, so did their status, to that of lower middle class. Those boyhood years were largely uneventful. Young Charles enjoyed listening to the frightening tales told by his nanny and displayed a taste for acting. From an early age, he also acquired a passionate love of reading, voraciously devouring eighteenth-century novels.

The most important incident of Dickens's early life occurred in 1824, when he was twelve years old. His parents' financial difficulties precipitated a series of traumatic experiences that dominated Dickens's youth and had an impact on the rest of his life. Young Dickens's education was abruptly interrupted when he was sent out to work in a blacking factory that made polish for shoes, stoves, and firegrates. Though miserable, he continued working there for several months, earning a pittance to help supplement the family's meager income. His father, John, was then arrested and imprisoned for debt—a common practice in accordance with the law of the time. John Dickens was joined in the Marshalsea prison by his family, except for Charles, who rented a room in a shabby boardinghouse near the factory. After some months John Dickens managed to pay off his debts, so he and his family could leave prison. Charles was able to stop working at the factory and return to school, thereby resuming a more normal life.

In the Victorian era, it was not uncommon for young children to be sent out to work, to be exploited by employers in ways that would be condemned today as cruel and inhuman. Children dragged heavy loads of coal through mine tunnels and endured intolerable conditions in mills and factories; young boys were forced to climb up chimneys as chimney sweeps. Only in 1833 was the Factory Act passed to reform working conditions: this law made it illegal to employ boys under the age of nine and curtailed the length of the work day to twelve hours (plus one and a half hours allocated for meals). Subsequent Factory Acts, passed in 1840, 1864, and 1875, together with other legislation, gradually improved the lot of workers, especially children. In contrast to what other child laborers had to endure, young Dickens's short term of employment in the blacking factory was tolerable, even comfortable. However, Dickens came from a middle- to lower-middle-class background: In class-conscious England, working in a factory could not easily be dismissed or forgotten.

By the time that Charles returned to school, the damage to the sensitive young boy was already done. He felt ashamed, humiliated, and socially disgraced. He also felt abandoned by both his father and his mother. Norman and Jeanne MacKenzie analyze the significance of what had happened:

> The domestic disaster was both unforgettable and unmentionable. As Dickens grew up he became eager for success and security, and he quickly acquired the manners of a gentleman. Yet he remained compulsively fascinated by this suppressed experience. It had forged an indissoluble bond of sympathy, even of identity, with the homeless, the friendless, the orphans, the hungry, the uneducated, and even the prisoners of London's lower depths. His childhood had been lost there and all his wanderings were a search for it.[9]

Many years later, when Dickens began writing novels, he

recollected his earlier life experiences and reworked them in fictional form. The events that occurred when he was twelve years old provided a rich source of inspiration and taught him empathy for the suffering of others. These events left their mark on most of his novels. Orphans and desperately unhappy children are commonplace in Dickens's works, particularly in *Oliver Twist, Nicholas Nickleby,* and *Great Expectations.* Imprisonment for debt is depicted in *Bleak House* and *Little Dorrit.* And the incident in the blacking factory appears, in a fictionalized version, in Dickens's autobiographical novel, *David Copperfield.*

Despite the enormous popularity and undisputed success that Dickens enjoyed in later life, the events that occurred when he was twelve—both his working in the blacking factory and his father's imprisonment for debt—inflicted psychological wounds that never completely healed. Biographers agree that Dickens's lifelong anxiety and insecurity can be traced back to these traumatic boyhood experiences. Instead of the justifiable pride and confidence that Dickens was entitled to feel as a self-made man who had raised himself from the lower classes entirely by his own efforts, he was haunted by recurrent feelings of inadequacy that seemed to undermine all that he had achieved.

CLERK AND REPORTER

In 1827, when Dickens was fifteen, his father could no longer afford to pay the school fees at Wellington House, so once again young Dickens had to go out to work. He spent the next two years working as a clerk in various legal offices. Familiarity with the law and its complex bureaucracy made Dickens contemptuous of both lawyers and the administrative apparatus of the antiquated British legal system. However, the experiences that Dickens endured, boring and frustrating as they were, again provided a rich source of material for subsequent novels. The descriptions of legal firms and clerks recur in his works; but the most extensive use by Dickens of his legal experiences is to be found in *Bleak House.* One of the masterpieces of his middle years, it mercilessly exposes the evils of the corrupt legal system, exacerbating (and reflecting) the public outrage that subsequently led to parliamentary reform of the law and its bureaucracy.

In 1830 Dickens, now eighteen, was no longer working as a legal clerk. Through the influence of his father, Dickens found occasional employment reporting parliamentary debates. He quickly mastered shorthand. He also rapidly became disillusioned with Parliament and with the antics of its members, who promised much but procrastinated and produced little.

In the same year, Dickens fell in love with Maria Beadnell, the youngest daughter of a banker. Young as he was, he contemplated marriage to Maria, regarding himself as an eligible suitor. The Beadnells welcomed Dickens into their home for their frequent social evenings, but aware of his father's previous bankruptcy and his own limited financial prospects as a parliamentary reporter, they did not consider him a suitable match for their daughter. The Beadnells discouraged further intimacy by sending their daughter on an extended visit to France, and when Maria returned home, she was no longer interested in resuming her relationship with Dickens. Angry and humiliated, Dickens deeply resented Maria's capricious behavior. Biographers suggest that her rejection reinforced his feelings of inadequacy.

Once again Dickens exploited his life experiences in novels written many years later. His disillusioned contempt for Parliament and its corruption became a major theme in *Bleak House* (together with his criticism of the iniquitous English legal system). Dickens's romance with Maria Beadnell became the model for a fictionalized version portrayed in *Great Expectations*, in the love of the lower-class Pip for the superior and condescending Estella.

It was not difficult for Dickens to shift from parliamentary to newspaper reporting. In 1834, at the age of twenty-two, he became a political reporter for the *Morning Chronicle*, an anti-Tory (anti-Conservative) newspaper with the second-largest circulation in Britain.

FIRST PUBLISHED WORKS

In the same year Dickens began writing sketches for his newspaper under the pen name of "Boz." A new career thus began. The owners of the *Morning Chronicle* founded a second newspaper, the *Evening Chronicle*, and an editor requested Dickens to write a series of miscellaneous articles by Boz.

Meanwhile, Dickens became involved in a new romance, this time with Catherine "Kate" Hogarth, daughter of one of the editors of the *Evening Chronicle*. Described as quiet, kindly, and good-natured, Hogarth had a restful personality. Her family welcomed Dickens as a suitor, and it was not long before the young couple became formally engaged.

At this stage Dickens returned to parliamentary reporting while simultaneously prowling the streets of London to find material for his sketches by Boz. All his activities in 1835 resulted in the ambitious young journalist suffering total exhaustion—a condition with which Dickens would become increasingly familiar in the years to come. *Sketches by Boz*, a collection of pieces previously printed in newspapers, was published in book form early in 1836. It served as a test case for Dickens, enabling him to assess the public's response to his writing. The work was so well received that, within a month, he was working on a new set of sketches to be entitled *The Posthumous Papers of the Pickwick Club*. Whereas *Sketches by Boz* was largely based on actual incidents witnessed by Dickens on the streets of London, the Pickwick sketches were completely fictional. They recounted Mr. Pickwick's stagecoach journey through the countryside, describing the scenes witnessed and the characters encountered on his travels. The Pickwick sketches were episodic in character; accordingly, they were ideally suited to the experimental publishing method of serialization, in which a new chapter or part of a chapter was published and sold separately each month.

Amid these exciting events, there was yet another. In April 1836 Dickens and Catherine Hogarth were married. On their return to London, after a week of honeymoon, they were joined in their home by Dickens's brother Frederick and Catherine's sister Mary Hogarth, both of whom became part of the new couple's household. As if Dickens were not busy enough, he then became involved in theatrical adaptations and negotiated further literary contracts.

A WRITER OF NOVELS

Early in 1837 the first installment of *Oliver Twist* was published. The economic background to the events portrayed in this novel was the Victorian practice of accommodating paupers in workhouses—poorhouses providing lodging and minimal sustenance. To ensure that no pauper abused this system, the inmates were subjected to extremely harsh conditions and compelled to endure the hardships imposed by petty bureaucrats. It is difficult to believe that Parliament had actually approved this system in 1834 in the Poor Law Amendment Act. In the novel, the young orphan, Oliver Twist, is shown suffering the cruel privation of the workhouse. After he leaves there, his life becomes a nightmare of horrors as he is forced into the criminal underworld of London. Fred Kaplan, commenting on the aspects of Victorian life portrayed in the novel, alludes to the "criminality, prostitution, child abuse, poverty, violence, and brutalization that urbanization has made a fulcrum of modern life."[10] The stark reality so graphically depicted in *Oliver Twist* was very different from the light-hearted humorous tone of *The Pickwick Papers*, but nonetheless its serialized installments sold well.

Enjoying great success as a young author, Dickens rapidly became a social celebrity. Tragedy, however, was quick to follow. One evening, without any warning, his beloved young sister-in-law Mary Hogarth collapsed and died the next day. Dickens was so grief-stricken that his monthly serial installment could not be published that month.

In 1838 Dickens began writing a new serial novel, *Nicholas Nickleby*, in which he exposed the abuses and brutality prevalent in Yorkshire boarding schools to which unwanted, often illegitimate boys were sent. The novel also contained general criticism of the wretched educational system of the day. The publication of the first installment of *Nicholas Nickleby* attested to Dickens's ever increasing popularity and prestige as a writer: fifty thousand copies were sold. Meanwhile, the final installment of *Oliver Twist* was published, and immediately afterward, it was published in hard cover as a complete novel. Even Queen Victoria read and commended *Oliver Twist.*

Dickens then went on to publish a collection of stories in his new weekly magazine *Master Humphrey's Clock.* Although the first issue in 1840 was popular, selling nearly seventy thousand copies, sales of the second issue decreased. To revive these flagging sales, Dickens abandoned his original plans for the magazine. Instead of stories, he published a serialized novel, *The Old Curiosity Shop*, a work that proved to be very popular with his readers. In describing the plight of Little Nell and her elderly grandfather, Dickens used the devices of melodrama so beloved by Victorians. Dickens's portrayal of Little Nell revealed his talent for evoking childhood; his dramatization of her death showed his genius for pathos. For the episode recounting her sad demise, readership soared, with one hundred thousand copies of this installment being sold.

AN AMERICAN TOUR AND ITS AFTERMATH

Dickens had for some time been contemplating a visit to the United States, and early in 1842 he embarked on the transatlantic voyage, which took eighteen days on a ship using both sail and steam. When he landed in Boston, Dickens was warmly welcomed, and he was then lionized and feted during his stay in that city. Elsewhere, too, he was honored with banquets and gala dinners. However, delighted as he was by his reception in America, Dickens was indignant at being deprived of the royalties to which he felt he was entitled for the American publication of his novels. At a banquet in his honor in Hartford, Connecticut, he angrily deplored the lack of an international copyright to protect writers. Dickens was nonetheless welcomed by frenzied crowds in New Haven, Connecticut, and New York, but the contentious issue of the international copyright continued to be a source of stress to him.

Visits to Philadelphia and Washington, D.C., followed, even though Dickens was becoming increasingly disenchanted with the manners and vulgarity of his American hosts, particularly their habit of chewing and spitting out tobacco. Above all, he loathed slavery. Dickens visited many other American cities until his departure from New York brought the exhausting trip to a welcome close.

On Dickens's return to England, he campaigned for recognition of the international copyright even as his quarrel with the American press over this issue became increasingly acrimonious. Toward the end of 1842 Dickens's book on his tour of America, *American Notes*, was published to poor, even hostile reviews in the American press. With the United States visit still fresh in his mind, he started working on a new novel, *Martin Chuzzlewit*, featuring a young hero who emigrates from Britain to America. Dickens had difficulty in writing much of this novel, and the work failed to appeal to his readers. His British sales dropped, and the American reviews were unfavorable.

RETURN TO ENGLAND

When Dickens returned to England from America in mid-1842, it was inevitable that he would view his country with new insight. What he saw occasioned little joy, for he con-

fronted a nation in which many suffered hunger and privation, one in which the masses were forced to live in
crowded, unsanitary, and disease-ridden urban slums as the
countryside became increasingly industrialized. The dis-
contented populace cried out for all to hear, but Parliament
remained obdurate, determined to resist and suppress the
widespread demand for reform. Dickens immediately became involved in agitation for reform, utilizing both his
journalistic and literary skills.

Since neither *American Notes* nor *Martin Chuzzlewit* gen-
erated much income, Dickens set about restoring his dwin-
dling fortune. To this end, he began writing *A Christmas
Carol*. Its theme is the transformation and redemption of the
miserly Scrooge by Tiny Tim, the crippled child of his em-
ployee. It was ready for sale by Christmas, deliberately timed
to ensure its popularity, though the financial proceeds were
not as great as Dickens had hoped. Within a year Dickens had
written another Christmas story, *The Chimes*, while on an extended stay in Italy with his family. It, too, was eagerly purchased by a public appreciative of Dickens's moral tale of the
virtuous poor oppressed by the rich. Both *A Christmas Carol*
and *The Chimes* expressed Dickens's belief in personal benevolence and its power to alleviate the suffering of the poor.

After returning to England from Italy, Dickens, often restless, once again became involved in journalistic enter-
prises—both a weekly magazine and a daily liberal newspaper. The projected magazine, to be entitled *The Cricket*,
eventually became instead another Christmas tale, *The
Cricket on the Hearth*, which sold even more copies than the
two previous Christmas books. Plans for the newspaper
were temporarily postponed while, throughout 1845, Dickens and his friends were busy staging amateur theatricals.
Toward the end of that year, financial arrangements were
completed for the funding of a liberal newspaper, the *Daily
News*. The first edition appeared early in the new year with
Dickens as editor. However, in spite of his initial enthusiasm,
he resigned after three weeks, pleased to rid himself of the
editorial burdens.

THE GREAT NOVELS OF HIS MATURITY

Free of the newspaper, Dickens became involved in the
scheme devised by the wealthy philanthropist, Angela
Burdett-Coutts, to found a home for fallen women in London

to be called Urania Cottage. He also began writing a new novel, *Dombey and Son*, in which elements of his current preoccupations—fallen women, family relations, money—appear as themes. Meanwhile, Dickens published yet another Christmas tale, *The Battle of Life*, about sacrificing for love, after which he and his family departed for Paris for the winter. He returned to London in the spring, and there he busied himself with his usual frenetic round of activities that included house hunting, producing charity theatricals, organizing the home for wayward women, and continuing to write installments of *Dombey and Son.*

In 1848 revolution erupted in France, reverberating across Europe. Some Englishmen supported it, but others, like Dickens, feared that the British liberal and democratic movements would precipitate a revolution in England, leading to bloodshed and anarchy. The Chartist movement, a precursor of the modern labor union that was formed to seek redress for workers' grievances and to secure universal male suffrage in England, was regarded as particularly dangerous, and Dickens distanced himself from such radical reform groups.

Immediately after completing *Dombey and Son* in 1848, Dickens resumed charitable work and the production of amateur theatricals. After many months of happy activity, he began writing a new Christmas story entitled *The Haunted Man*. The death of his sister Fanny and various other incidents revived memories of childhood events that he normally preferred to forget—his family's bankruptcy, his work in the blacking factory, the family's sojourn in Marshalsea prison—and some of these recollections surfaced in *The Haunted Man*, with its theme of forgetting unhappy memories of the past.

Recollections of the past led to Dickens beginning work early in 1849 on what was to be one of his greatest and best-loved novels, *David Copperfield*. Narrated in the first-person by the adult David Copperfield as his autobiography, the book traces the growth and development of a writer—a variation of the bildungsroman, or novel of development. Indeed, Philip Collins points out that "since its hero becomes a novelist, it is . . . a 'Portrait of an Artist as a Young Man.'"[11] As critics have frequently noted, the work is also a fictionalized reworking of some of the events of Dickens's own life. Trevor Blount, for example, maintains: "Its autobiographic content is unmistakable, and there is the inevitable feeling that we

are being privileged to come closer in this work than elsewhere to Dickens the man: that in a way David is Dickens."[12]
The first installment was published in May of that year. On
completion in 1850, *David Copperfield* was acclaimed by
both the public and critics. While still writing installments of
the novel, Dickens established a weekly magazine entitled
Household Words. The first issue appeared early in 1850,
with one hundred thousand copies sold. Although sales subsequently dropped, the magazine still made a profit and continued to be published for the next nine years.

Early in 1852 Dickens arranged for the publication of the
first installment of *Bleak House*, another novel that proved to
be among his greatest works. Robert Alan Donovan praises
Bleak House in the highest terms: "What makes it a monu-
mental artistic achievement is that it is . . . one of the most
powerful indictments of a heartless and irresponsible society
ever written."[13] Dickens's outraged exposé of the cruel practices and blatant corruption of the Court of Chancery, the
highest law court in nineteenth-century England, coincided
with popular loathing of this outmoded bureaucratic institution that had come to epitomize a travesty of justice. Indeed,
the Chancery Reform Act was tabled in Parliament toward
the end of 1851. *Bleak House* attacked many of the abuses and
iniquities of the period, ranging from the stranglehold of the
upper classes on Parliament to the hideous squalor of the
disease-ridden slums of London. The relentless onslaught
against injustice, however, dominated the novel and was dramatized in the narratives of those characters who had fallen
victim to the court's fatal clutches. Tens of thousands of readers eagerly bought each installment of the serialized novel.

Incredibly, even while writing the monthly serials of
Bleak House and editing *Household Words,* Dickens still
found time to devote to charitable causes. He undertook exhausting tours of his amateur theatricals to raise money for
struggling writers. This busy year also included a two-week
vacation in France. Not surprisingly, the year 1852 ended
with Dickens suffering from exhaustion.

Soon after Dickens completed the last installment of
Bleak House, he began writing another novel, *Hard Times*, to
be published serially in 1854 in *Household Words.* The new
novel immediately helped boost the magazine's diminishing
circulation. Commenting on *Hard Times*, Edgar H. Johnson
notes: "It is an analysis and a condemnation of the ethos of

industrialism."[14] The work is a harsh indictment of the deplorable conditions suffered by workers in Coketown, where industrial pollution blights the landscape. *Hard Times* is also well known for dramatizing Jeremy Bentham's theory of utilitarianism, in which value is assigned according to utility, as well as for satirizing the pedagogic view that propounds the teaching of facts to the total exclusion of the creative imagination.

THE CRIMEAN WAR

In March 1854 England and France declared war on Russia, allying themselves with Turkey. The incredible incompetence of Parliament was never more dramatically revealed than in its bureaucratic bungling and callous indifference to the suffering of British soldiers fighting in Russia during the Crimean War. At the same time England was ravaged by an epidemic of cholera that killed thousands. Even one of Dickens's daughters was afflicted, but she fortunately survived, having contracted a milder strain of the disease.

Toward the end of the year Dickens was engaged in producing theatrical productions as usual, now interspersed with public readings of his books. The end of year festivities were muted by the disastrous news emerging from the Russian front: Wounds, disease, and the severe Russian winter had decimated the British troops, making most British soldiers casualties of the war. Public outrage culminated in the resignation of the prime minister, Lord Aberdeen (George Hamilton-Gordon), and the defeat of the liberal Whig Party then in power in Parliament.

It was during the Crimean War that the redoubtable Florence Nightingale intervened in the management of the British military hospital established in Scutari, Turkey. Shocked by the appalling filth and neglect of the wounded, she and her trained female nursing staff introduced strict hygienic standards, helped reduce mortality figures, and proved beyond any doubt that nursing was a medically skilled and honorable profession. Dickens and his philanthropist associate, Angela Burdett-Coutts, assisted Nightingale by buying medical equipment for the hospital.

THE WOMEN IN DICKENS'S LIFE

In February 1855 Dickens received an unexpected letter from Maria Beadnell, whom he had once loved as a young man. When he received the letter, several decades after Maria had rejected him, all the memories of that relationship resurfaced, and the two exchanged a number of highly emotional letters in which they arranged an intimate reunion prior to their having dinner together with their spouses. However, their meeting proved to be a shattering disappointment to Dickens since the reality of the middle-aged Maria Winter was very different from Dickens's romantic fantasy of the lovely young Maria Beadnell from his past. The dinner had to be politely endured, as did several subsequent social engagements, but Dickens was relieved when the families parted and went their separate ways.

In the course of 1855, Dickens began a new serial novel entitled *Little Dorrit*, the first installment of which was published in December of that year. In this novel he recalled the period in his youth when his father was imprisoned for debt in the Marshalsea prison. Indeed, as Philip Hobsbaum argues, "the prison proves to be a microcosm of the society outside."[15] This experience was fictionalized in the novel in Dickens's detailed description of the incarceration in the Marshalsea of Little Dorrit's father, William. Critics have repeatedly pointed out that the concept of imprisonment, recurrent throughout the work, is not only literal but symbolic, not only realistic but psychological.

During this period Dickens purchased Gad's Hill Place, a famous historical mansion, mentioned in Shakespeare's *Henry* IV, that Dickens remembered admiring in childhood. By mid-1857 Dickens and his family had moved in, a date coinciding with the completion of *Little Dorrit*. Immediately afterward, Dickens was once again involved in a hectic round of theatrical activity and public readings from his novels. Among the plays performed was *The Frozen Deep*, a melodrama written by his friend William Wilkie Collins. Its theme was that of self-sacrifice for a friend, its setting an Arctic expedition. This play was scheduled to be performed in an enormous hall in Manchester, among other places, and professional actresses were engaged for the female roles. The Ternan family was hired—the mother, Frances Eleanor, and two of her daughters, Maria and Ellen. Dickens fell in love with Ellen Ternan, the youngest daughter. Biographers suggest that she reminded him of Maria Beadnell and Mary Hogarth (his dead sister-in-law)—the lost loves of his youth.

Dickens's obsession with Ellen Ternan brought to a crisis

his dissatisfaction with Catherine, his wife of twenty-one years. Catherine's parents, the Hogarths, were outraged when they discovered that Dickens was estranged from their daughter, and he in turn was angered by their interference. During the Victorian era, secular divorce was rare, granted only on the grounds of the adultery of either spouse, or cruelty, or desertion by the husband. Divorce was not a viable option for the Dickenses. Because of his reputation, Dickens feared the effect of marital scandal and so was reluctant to publicly announce his separation from Catherine in 1858. He sought distraction in a series of paid public readings of his works after having seen the immense popularity of his readings for charity. Besides, he had to have some means of paying for his extravagant purchase of Gad's Hill Place.

The separation of Dickens and his wife was not made public until an incident occurred that humiliated Catherine. A bracelet that Dickens purchased as a gift for Ternan was erroneously delivered to Catherine instead. She immediately accused her husband of being involved in an illicit love affair even though he protested his innocence, maintaining that the bracelet was intended to be no more than a memento for Ternan of their having acted together on stage. At this point, Catherine's family intervened and the situation got out of hand. The Hogarths spread gossip about Dickens, and he in turn issued a demand for a public apology from them. The affair reached a new low when Dickens published a newspaper article vilifying Catherine and praising Ternan, although the actress was not mentioned by name. Dickens and Catherine were never reconciled, nor were they ever divorced; they remained separated for the rest of their lives. It is particularly ironic that the writer who celebrated the joy of domestic harmony in his fiction should himself disrupt his family by initiating the separation from his wife and taking a mistress, however discreetly.

Catherine's sister Georgina, who had been the housekeeper for many years, remained in Dickens's household. Except for one son, Charley, the children all chose to live with their father, leaving Catherine bereft of her family. After his separation from his wife, Dickens quarreled with a number of his friends who, he felt, had not shown him sufficient loyalty or support. Among these were William Bradbury and Frederick Evans, shareholders in the periodical *Household Words*. Dickens established a rival magazine in

1859 entitled *All the Year Round,* and after a legal dispute, he also acquired control of *Household Words.*

LATER NOVELS

To ensure the success of *All the Year Round,* Dickens began writing a new novel to be serialized in the magazine. The novel, *A Tale of Two Cities,* proved to be among his most popular. Set during the previous century, at the time of the French Revolution, it was strongly influenced by British historian and author Thomas Carlyle's study of that period. The political views conveyed by the novel emphasize that even though the revolution in France resulted from the oppression of the lower classes by the aristocracy, the mob was not an instrument of justice but an uncontrollable force that wreaked violence, destruction, and anarchy. Interwoven with this political theme was the melodrama of self-sacrifice for a friend, recalling the plot of Wilkie Collins's drama *The Frozen Deep,* in which Dickens had acted several years earlier.

All the Year Round constantly required new material for publication. Following *A Tale of Two Cities,* Wilkie Collins's novel *The Woman in White* was published in the magazine in installments during 1860 and sold very well. Seeking fresh material, Dickens approached two leading contemporary novelists, George Eliot (Mary Anne Evans) and Elizabeth Gaskell. However, both declined his offer to publish their works in his magazine since neither was comfortable with the hectic pressures of serialization.

If *All the Year Round* was to continue publication, Dickens himself had to come to its rescue. Accordingly he began what was to prove his most beloved and perennially popular novel, *Great Expectations,* the first installment of which was published in late 1860. The structure of *Great Expectations* was tighter than that of his previous novels; there were no diversions or lengthy asides so the plot advanced rapidly, with increasing dramatic tension. Nonetheless, the novel displays Dickens's characteristic motifs—the hero as orphan, the prisoner figure, class conflicts, mysterious events, coincidences, bizarre occurrences, and eccentric characters. Throughout the novel Dickens dramatizes the themes of money and class mobility with an elegance not found in his previous works. H.M. Daleski notes that a major theme in the novel is "the corrupting power of wealth."[16] *Great Expectations* is also a superb example of that great nineteenth-century literary genre, the bildungsroman, or novel of development, in which a young man progresses from the errors of youth to self-knowledge and the wisdom of maturity. *Great Expectations* follows in the tradition of *David Copperfield*, Dickens's previous experiment in this genre. Dickens completed writing the novel by mid-1861 and soon afterward plunged into preparations for public readings of novels to be given later that year. These readings were, as always, incredibly successful and continued over a period of eight months.

The next project Dickens undertook was the Christmas story for that year, *Mrs. Lirriper's Lodgings*, of which more than 200,000 copies were sold. He then began writing a new novel, *Our Mutual Friend*, which commenced serial publication early in 1864. Before that novel was completed, Dickens, returning from Paris with Ellen Ternan, was involved in a serious train accident. He managed to climb out of the window of his railroad car only to discover that, having left the manuscript of *Our Mutual Friend* behind, he had to clamber back inside in order to retrieve it. A novel with a complex plot, *Our Mutual Friend* focuses on money, corruption, and mercenary behavior. J. Hillis Miller emphasizes that "never does Dickens so concentrate his attention on the power of money as in this last of his completed novels."[17] At its center are the heaps of household rubbish, the tainted source of the money that dominates and blights the lives of so many of the characters portrayed. The final chapters were completed toward the end of 1865, followed by Dickens's customary Christmas story, *Dr. Marigold's Prescriptions*, which Dickens read publicly and which sold more than 250,000 copies.

READING TOURS IN AMERICA AND ENGLAND

Dickens then proceeded to give an extended series of popular readings. Meanwhile, he was becoming increasingly tempted by an invitation to undertake a lucrative reading tour of America. To be sure, he was aware that his tours of Britain were becoming increasingly exhausting and at times feared that his health was being threatened by incessant travel and frequent performances. He was worried that the inevitable strain of a reading tour of America would be exacerbated by the vastness of the continent. However, he was offered so vast a sum of money that it was difficult to refuse.

Having experienced poverty and family bankruptcy as a child, Dickens never felt completely secure financially. Moreover, although he was now wealthy, his expenses were correspondingly high, and he was also concerned about the financial prospects of his sons. In short, he felt that he could never have too much money.

After ascertaining that there seemed to be no lingering resentment in America from his previous visit there, Dickens decided to proceed with his American tour. He arrived in Boston in November 1867 and was accorded a riotous welcome at his readings. The New York public greeted him with the same enthusiasm, but his enjoyment of these lively, popular public readings was interrupted by bouts of illness. Even before he set sail for America, Dickens was in denial about his health, which worsened during his American tour. He frequently drove himself to exhaustion, and neither diet nor medication brought about any real improvement. His tour continued in city after city across the vastness of America as he endured winter weather much more severe than he had experienced in England. Despite all these tribulations, Dickens had a remarkable capacity to overcome his physical weakness as soon as he stepped onto the stage and began his performance. There were welcome periods of rest and social activities, yet throughout his performances and his attendance at banquets and parties, Dickens suffered an underlying weariness. He concluded his final performances in Boston and New York with gracious farewell speeches, vowing to append his revised opinion of America to future editions of *American Notes* and *Martin Chuzzlewit.* He was now full of praise for the American people and for their great country—a bastion of freedom. Dickens earned a great deal of money on his American tour, and by the end of the voyage home, his health seemed to be restored.

Dickens was greeted with flags and festivities on his return to England but was soon caught up in a busy schedule of writing, editing, and administrative duties, in addition to family responsibilities. He was soon negotiating a new round of public readings in England, once again minimizing his health problems and ignoring the warnings of his friends that the strain of constant travel and frequent stage performances was destroying him. However, once he actually began another public reading tour, he was forced to acknowledge that he longed for it to be over.

On this reading tour, Dickens strained after sensational-ism more than ever before, dramatically rendering the two scenes of horror in *Oliver Twist* in which Bill Sikes murders Nancy and is then hanged accidentally while fleeing from the police. Such scenes traumatized the audience, driving them to the verge of hysteria, and proved no less traumatic to Dickens himself. Those who witnessed the murder and subsequent hanging enacted on the stage were struck by Dickens's remarkable talent; indeed, some averred that what they had witnessed was not a reading but rather acting of enormous intensity. Some critics went even further, as-serting that Dickens paid a heavy price by expending his own life's vitality while acting out these scenes from the novel on the stage.

FINAL ILLNESS AND DEATH

Dickens's health markedly deteriorated, and in February 1869 he became ill. Performances had to be canceled, but even after consulting a doctor, Dickens continued to deny the seriousness of his condition. Though urged to rest, he re-peatedly ignored this advice. When his assistant attempted to persuade him to cease performing the scenes from *Oliver Twist* that were so stressful, Dickens still persisted in doing so until two eminent doctors warned him of impending paralysis should he continue his stage appearances. Dickens was a poor patient, always convinced that he would fully re-cover his health and constantly pressuring his doctors to agree to the resumption of his readings. A compromise was reached at last, and Dickens agreed to curtail what he reluc-tantly conceded would be his final tour.

Within a few months Dickens seemed to have recovered his health, sufficiently so to contemplate a tour of Australia that he had once turned down. Fortunately, common sense prevailed, but it was not long before he was caught up in his usual whirl of social activities. By midyear Dickens was planning a new novel, *The Mystery of Edwin Drood*, to be published in installments. In the new year, which was to prove his last, Dickens gave his farewell series of public readings to audiences that gave him a tumultuous welcome and enthusiastic applause. At his final reading, he gave a brief but moving speech of farewell to an audience of more than two thousand and then left the stage with tears in his eyes. There followed a series of farewell dinners with the notables of London and even an invitation to an audience with Queen Victoria.

Dickens continued working on the installments of *The Mystery of Edwin Drood* and returned to his beloved Gad's Hill Place, but his last novel was never completed. He died on June 9, 1870. His coffin was transported to London, where he was accorded the rare honor, reserved for the greatest of the land, of burial in Westminster Abbey. In his will, Dickens requested that he not be commemorated with either monuments or memorials. Instead, he says, "I rest my claims to the remembrance of my country upon my published works . . ."[18]

NOTES

1. John Forster, *The Life of Charles Dickens*, vol. 1. New York: Dutton, 1980, p. 3.

2. T.W. Heyck, *The Transformation of Intellectual Life in Victorian England*, ed. Richard Price. London: Croom Helm, 1982, p. 26.

3. Philip Collins, "Dickens and His Readers," in *Victorian Values: Personalities and Perspectives in Nineteenth-Century Society*, ed. Gordon Marsden. New York: Longman, 1990, p. 56.

4. Gordon Marsden, ed., *Victorian Values: Personalities and Perspectives in Nineteenth-Century Society*. New York: Longman, 1990, p. 44.

5. Heyck, *The Transformation of Intellectual Life*, pp. 25–26. These figures have been extrapolated from Heyck's statistics.

6. Marsden, *Victorian Values*, p. 44.

7. Walter E. Houghton, *The Victorian Frame of Mind, 1830–1870*. New Haven, CT: Yale University Press, 1975, pp. 274–75.

8. Robert Alan Donovan, "Structure and Idea in *Bleak House*," in *The Victorian Novel: Modern Essays in Criticism*, ed. Ian Watt. New York: Oxford University Press, 1971, p. 83.

9. Norman and Jeanne MacKenzie, *Dickens: A Life*. New York: Oxford University Press, 1979, pp. 16–17.

10. Fred Kaplan, ed., *Charles Dickens: "Oliver Twist."* New York: W.W. Norton, 1993, p. ix.

11. Philip Collins, *Charles Dickens: "David Copperfield."* London: Edward Arnold, 1977, p. 14.

12. Trevor Blount, introduction to *The Personal History of David Copperfield*, by Charles Dickens. New York: Penguin, 1979, pp. 16–17.

13. Donovan, "Structure and Idea in *Bleak House*," p. 108.

14. Edgar H. Johnson, "Critique of Materialism," in *Twentieth Century Interpretations of "Hard Times,"* ed. Paul Edward Gray. Englewood Cliffs, NJ: Prentice-Hall, 1969, p. 48.

15. Philip Hobsbaum, *A Reader's Guide to Charles Dickens.* London: Thames and Hudson, 1972, p. 189.

16. H.M. Daleski, *Dickens and the Art of Analogy.* London: Faber and Faber, 1970, p. 237.

17. J. Hillis Miller, "*Our Mutual Friend,*" in *Dickens: A Collection of Critical Essays,* ed. Martin Price. Englewood Cliffs, NJ: Prentice-Hall, 1967, p. 169.

18. Quoted in John Forster, *The Life of Charles Dickens,* vol. 2. New York: Dutton, 1980, p. 422.

CHAPTER 1

FORMATIVE INFLUENCES ON DICKENS'S EARLY LIFE

CHARLES DICKENS

The Boy in the Blacking Factory

Edgar Johnson

Edgar Johnson, professor of English at the City University of New York, is recognized as a distinguished authority on Dickens. Johnson's two-volume definitive biography of the writer received universal critical acclaim. In this extract from his biography, Johnson analyzes the most traumatic episode of Dickens's childhood, one so mortifying that he kept it secret for most of his adult life. This unfortunate experience involved his family's financial difficulties, his father's arrest for debt, and John Dickens's subsequent imprisonment in the Marshalsea Prison, where he was joined by his family (except for young Charles). Equally mortifying to the twelve-year-old Charles was being sent to work in a blacking factory. Dickens felt utterly outcast and abandoned by his parents; he was ashamed of the disgrace to his family and to himself. In class-conscious Victorian England, the whole experience scarred Dickens for life, even though it only lasted for a few months.

It should be noted that when Johnson repeatedly refers to Dickens's own account of these childhood events, Johnson is actually quoting from the autobiographical fragment which Dickens gave to his friend John Forster and which Forster published in his own biography of the writer.

Events were soon to stab [young Charles Dickens] with a sharper and more personal anguish. It came, ironically enough, through the kindly intentions of James Lamert [a boarder and friend of the Dickens family]. He had ceased to live with the Dickens family before they left Camden Town, but knowing how things were going with them and seeing how Charles was employed from day to day, he made a helpful suggestion. . . . "In an evil hour for me," Dickens felt, James Lamert now proposed that Charles should make himself useful in the blacking warehouse, at a salary of six shillings a week. During the dinner hour, from twelve to one, he would even give the lad some school lessons every day.

DICKENS'S BETRAYAL BY HIS PARENTS

His father and mother accepted the offer very willingly, and on a Monday morning only two days after his twelfth birthday Charles started to work. The event had come upon him with the suddenness of unforeseen catastrophe; and it left him stunned, sick with despair. "It is wonderful to me," he says, "how I could have been so easily cast away at such an age. It is wonderful to me, that, even after my descent into the poor little drudge I had been since we came to London, no one had compassion enough on me—a child of singular abilities, quick, eager, delicate, and soon hurt, bodily or mentally—to suggest that something might have been spared, as certainly it might have been, to place me at any common school. Our friends, I take it, were tired out. No one made any sign. My father and mother were quite satisfied. They could hardly have been more so, if I had been twenty years of age, distinguished at a grammar-school, and going to Cambridge."

It is the shock and bitterness of a hurt child, of course, that speaks in these words—a child so deeply wounded that the hurt is still there, a quarter of a century later, when they were spoken. But if the patience of the family's friends was exhausted, it was hardly to be expected that they should single out one of the Dickens children and offer to be responsible for him. No doubt his harassed parents were thankful enough for James Lamert's well-meant and kindly offer, but they were hardly apt to look upon it or any other aspect of their plight with complacency. Their income was entirely devoured in the endeavor to deal with their debts; and, besides Charles and Fanny, there were four helpless younger children in the family, from Letitia, who was eight, down to two-year-old Alfred Lamert. Nor was there anything unusual, even later at the end of the nineteenth century, in a boy going to work at twelve. The average school life for a child in the 1820's and for a considerable time thereafter was perhaps two years, perhaps eighteen months. Six shillings a week was no bad wage for a boy at the time, and the hours at the warehouse were not more prolonged than usual. They began at 8 A.M. and ended at 8 P.M., with a lapse of one hour for dinner and half an hour for tea. And despite the comic singing and the admiration of the boatbuilder at Limehouse Hole, neither John Dickens nor his wife suspected that their bright, small-bodied youngster would turn out to be a prodigy.

But in the self-absorbed grief of childhood, Charles hardly realized how frantic his parents were with anxiety, or what a relief even this provision for one of their children must be

"HOW MUCH I SUFFERED"

John Forster, a journalist and friend of Dickens, wrote the authoritative contemporary biography of the novelist. Dickens confided in Forster and even gave him an autobiographical manuscript describing his recollections of the traumatic events of his childhood. The following extract is from Dickens's manuscript, as quoted in Forster's famous two-volume biography, published only after Dickens's death.

"I know I do not exaggerate, unconsciously and unintentionally, the scantiness of my resources and the difficulties of my life. I know that if a shilling or so were given me by anyone, I spent it in a dinner or a tea. I know that I worked, from morning to night, with common men and boys, a shabby child. I know that I tried, but ineffectually, not to anticipate my money, and to make it last the week through by putting it away in a drawer I had in the counting-house, wrapped into six little parcels, each parcel containing the same amount, and labelled with a different day. I know that I have lounged about the streets, insufficiently and unsatisfactorily fed. I know that, but for the mercy of God, I might easily have been, for any care that was taken of me, a little robber or a little vagabond. . . .

"How much I suffered, it is . . . utterly beyond my power to tell. No man's imagination can overstep the reality. But I kept my own counsel, and I did my work. . . .

"My rescue from this kind of existence I considered quite hopeless, and abandoned as such, altogether; though I am solemnly convinced that I never, for one hour, was reconciled to it, or was otherwise than miserably unhappy. I felt keenly, however, the being so cut off from my parents, my brothers, and sisters."

John Forster, *The Life of Charles Dickens.* Vol. 1. New York: Dutton, 1980, pp. 25–26.

to them. The boy had an extraordinary desire to learn and distinguish himself, and to him this represented the end of all his hopes. Furthermore, John Dickens's pretensions had led his son to regard himself as a young gentleman, to whom this descent into drudging among common boys with uncouth manners was unspeakably humiliating. . . .

The birthplace of Charles Dickens in Portsmouth, England.

At first, to be sure, James Lamert made some effort to dissociate [Dickens] from the other boys and give him the noonday hour of daily instruction. The blacking warehouse was a crazy tumble-down old house abutting on the river at Hungerford Stairs. Dirty and decayed, its wainscoted rooms and rotten floors and staircase resounded with the squeaking and shuffling of the old gray rats swarming down in the cellars. Charles sat and worked by himself in a recess of the countinghouse, overlooking the coal barges and the river. His task was "to cover the pots of paste-blacking; first with a piece of oil-paper, and then with a bit of blue paper; to tie them round with a string; and then to clip the paper close and neat, all round, until it looked as smart as a pot of ointment from an apothecary's shop." On each of these, finally, he pasted a printed label.

But so inconvenient an arrangement of isolation soon died away, and so did the noon-hour teaching. His small work table, his grosses of pots, papers, string, scissors, paste-pot, and labels, vanished out of the countinghouse and moved downstairs to the common workroom. He was not so young as not to know that he would be slighted and despised if he could not work as well as the others, so despite his suffering he soon made himself as quick and skillful as the other boys. But there was a difference of conduct and manners between him and them that resulted in his being called, perhaps not quite reverentially, "the young gentleman.". . .

DICKENS FEELS HUMILIATED

"No words can express the secret agony of my soul," the autobiography goes on, "as I sunk into this companionship; compared these every day associates with those of my happier childhood; and felt my early hopes of growing up to be a learned and distinguished man, crushed in my breast. The deep remembrance of the sense I had of being utterly neglected and hopeless; of the shame I felt in my position; of the misery it was to my young heart to believe that, day by day, what I had learned, and thought, and delighted in, and raised my fancy and my emulation up by, was passing away from me, never to be brought back any more; cannot be written. My whole nature was so penetrated with the grief and humiliation of such considerations, that even now, famous and caressed and happy, I often forget in my dreams that I have a dear wife and children; even that I am a man; and wander desolately back to that time of my life."

But, in his pride, he bottled all his despair within his own breast. "I never said, to man or boy, how it was that I came to be there, or gave the least indication of being sorry that I was there. That I suffered in secret, and that I suffered exquisitely, no one ever knew but I."

DICKENS'S FATHER IS IMPRISONED FOR DEBT

Just eleven days later than the Monday on which Charles began his forlorn labors, his father was arrested at the suit of one James Karr for a debt of £40. The first three nights of his detention he was provided with lodgings in the sponging house maintained by the bailiff, while he tried to raise money and avoid being formally committed to prison. Charles, his eyes swollen with tears, spent the week-end running errands and carrying messages for the weeping prisoner. But all efforts were in vain: on Monday John Dickens was taken from the sponging house to the Marshalsea. His last words to the sorrowing lad as he entered the gates were that the sun had set upon him for ever, and they stabbed the boy with anguish. "I really believed at the time," Dickens said many years later, "that they had broken my heart.". . .

John Dickens could not lose his natural ornateness of utterance even in a debtors' prison, but he was dreadfully shaken. The consequences of his easy complacency had at last caught up with him. The failure of the long struggle since they had left Chatham, and the catastrophe of imprisonment, had overwhelmed him with the fear that he was utterly ruined. He became tremulously tragic; it may have been in John Dickens at this time that his son observed that fluttering and frightened motion of the fingers about the lips that he later attributed to [his character] William Dorrit in the same misfortune.

And there was reason enough to be frightened. There was no way in which he could pay his debts; he must either remain in prison or take advantage of the Insolvent Debtors' Act. He had been in the Navy Pay Office nineteen years, but a man who incurred the disgrace of insolvency could hardly hope to be retained there. In that case, income, pension possibilities, all hope, would vanish. . . .

THE FAMILY PAWNS ITS POSSESSIONS

Meanwhile Charles crept every hopeless day from Gower Street to the drudgery of Hungerford Stairs, and his dis-

tracted mother tried to keep things going and the whimper-
ing children fed by pawning brooches and spoons and gradually stripping the rooms bare of furniture. . . . At last there
was nothing left in Gower Street but a few chairs, a kitchen
table, and some beds; and the family camped out in the two
parlors of the emptied house. . . .

At Lady Day the encampment at Gower Street broke up;
the key was sent back to the landlord (who was very glad to
get it), and Mrs. Dickens and the younger children went to
live in the Marshalsea.

Dickens's Vision of the Child

Frank Donovan

Frank Donovan was a scriptwriter and film producer before becoming the author of over thirty books, most on American history. In this excerpt from his psychological study of Dickens, he contrasts the writer's idealized view of childhood to his fictional portrayals of children. In his imagination, Dickens envisages childhood as a happy and carefree stage of life. However, in his novels he seldom portrays a happy child: some children die young, others are cripples, and many are orphans. Most are poor and live sordid lives in the slums of London. Those who are not orphans are often subject to the cruelty of their schoolmasters. Even worse, many children suffer from parental neglect. The children in Dickens's novels generally find the adult world hostile and, at best, indifferent. Few have any sympathetic siblings or friends.

Biographers suggest that Dickens's preoccupation with these unhappy children springs from his own unfortunate experiences in childhood. His father neglected his son's education, while his mother arranged for young Dickens to return to work at the blacking factory even after he was dismissed. These events left an indelible mark on Dickens's attitude to life, shaping his vision of the child as shown in his novels.

There is great paradox involving Dickens' fictional children. In discussing childhood, as such, he always presented it as the most desirable stage of life—a time when "everything was happy." His works are replete with descriptions of gay children playing in an ideal, natural atmosphere, free from the cares and problems of the adult world and far from the

Frank Donovan, *The Children of Charles Dickens*. London: Leslie Frewin Publishers Ltd., 1969. Copyright © 1968 by Frank Donovan. Reproduced by permission.

unwholesome aspects of the squalid city. Typical of such an idyl is a passage from *Nicholas Nickleby* where Nicholas takes the dying Smike into the countryside and the boy reminisces about his youth in these delightful surroundings: "With what longing and enjoyment he would point out some tree that he had climbed a hundred times to peep at the birds in their nests, and then the branch from which he used to shout to little Kate, who stood below terrified. There is the old house with the tiny window through which the sun used to stream in and wake him in the summer mornings—*they* were all summer mornings then—and the very rosebush, a present from some little lover, and which she had planted with her own hands. There were the hedgerows in which they had so often gathered wild flowers together—it all came back upon the mind, as events of childhood do. Nothing in itself—perhaps a word, a laugh, a look, but better than the hardest words or severest sorrows of eye."

THE REALITY FOR CHILDREN

But when Dickens describes such a childhood it is usually in terms of something long lost, or something that might have been. Smike, when the reader first meets him, is in a bleak Yorkshire school where the lives of the students are a constant misery. Despite his emphasis on the happiness of childhood, it is hard to find a happy child in Dickens. The one adjective that applies to almost all of them is pathetic. Several of his child characters meet early deaths, some of them are cripples or otherwise shortchanged by nature. Those that are whole and live are usually buffeted in one way or another by the ill winds of fate. A very high percentage are orphans or half-orphans and are denied the stability of a loving home. Dickens wrote extensively about the charms of hearth and home, but with few exceptions—the Toodles children in *Dombey and Son,* the Cratchit youngsters in the *Christmas Carol,* the Kenwigs children in *Nicholas Nickleby,* and one or two others—none of his youngsters have such a home. Most of his children are maltreated, subject to sarcasm, bad temper, and restrictive convictions of parents or guardians—when they are not whipped, beaten, or kept in solitary confinement. Dickens extolls the charms of the country, but his little heroes and heroines are mostly left longing for such charms while they live their weary lives in the fetid streets, moldy dwellings, workhouses, or suppressive schools.

The bulk of the children are poor and of the lower class. Many were children of the London streets, surrounded by vice and filth, cruelty and neglect. The heart of Dickens the reformer was with such children; these were the youngsters who most needed the type of childhood which he eulogized when he wrote about childhood rather than children. Dickens understood such waifs—[British author] G.K. Chesterton summarized his grasp of the creatures of the slums by saying that Dickens had "the key to the street."

ORPHANED AND REJECTED

The orphans or half-orphans in Dickens' writing form an impressive list. Oliver Twist is an orphan, as are Noah Claypole and Fagin's band of young pickpockets in that book. Pip in *Great Expectations* is an orphan, as are Martin Chuzzlewit and Little Nell. In *David Copperfield* there are four juvenile orphans—Emily, Traddles, the Orfling, and Martha Endell—and six half-orphans; Dora and Agnes have no mother, and Heep, Ham, Steerforth, and David himself have no father. Barnaby Rudge is abandoned by his murdering father. The mother of the Dombey children dies at Paul's birth. . . .

Many of Dickens' children who are not orphaned are in a worse state because of cruel, neglectful, rejective, or oppressive parents, or surrogate parents, usually in the form of schoolmasters or schoolmistresses. In *Dombey and Son* he wrote: "Not an orphan in the world can be so deserted as the child who is an outcast from a living parent's love." In that book there are three parents who signally fail to discharge their responsibilities; in *Barnaby Rudge* there are five. One review of *Little Dorrit* commented on the "remarkable number of false and inadequate parents." *Nicholas Nickleby* is peopled entirely by unwanted children, "one huge indictment of the failure of parental responsibility." In one letter Dickens wrote that the greater number of parents who came under his observation seemed to him to be selfish in their behavior to their children.

ADULT INSENSITIVITY

To most of his children the adult world is vicious, hostile, uncomprehending, or indifferent. Typical of the parental background against which many of his children were raised is the recollection of Arthur Clennam in *Little Dorrit* of his upbringing: "Trained by main force; broken, not bent . . . I am the child of parents who weighed, measured, and priced everything . . . Austere faces, inexorable discipline, penance in this world and terror in the next—nothing graceful or gentle anywhere, and the void in my cowed heart everywhere—this was my childhood, if I may so misuse the word as to apply it to such a beginning of life."

Many of Dickens' fictional children who were not mistreated were often misunderstood. In a late essay he discoursed on the ill effects of not paying attention to childish beliefs and fancies: "It would be difficult to overstate the intensity and accuracy of an intelligent child's observation. At that impressible time of life, it must sometimes produce a fixed impression. If the fixed impression be of an object terrible to the child, it will be (for want of reasoning upon) inseparable from great fear. Force the child at such a time, be Spartan with it, send it into the dark against its will, leave it in a lonely bedroom against its will, and you had better murder it."

Dickens had ideas on child-rearing that were far in advance of his time. A modern child psychologist would heartily approve the sentiments of the above quotation, which Dickens pointed up in several novels by instances of the cruelty of "forcing" a child or ignoring its "silly" beliefs. In *Dombey and Son* Mrs. Pipchin would stand no nonsense from her little charges and used Spartan methods to correct it: "As little Miss Pankey was afraid of sleeping alone in the dark, Mrs. Pipchin always made it a point of driving her upstairs herself, like a sheep; and it was cheerful to hear Miss Pankey moaning long afterwards, in the least eligible chamber, and Mrs. Pipchin now and then going in to shake her."

Most of Dickens' children are lonely as well as neglected. Few had brothers or sisters and most of his heroes had no friends. Deprived of parental love, many of the youngsters were thrust out into an alien adult world to fend for themselves. Typical of the situation in which many Dickens' children found themselves is this description of Oliver Twist's feelings when he is captured by Fagin's minions: "Weak with recent illness; stupefied by the blows and the suddenness of the attack; terrified by the fierce growling of the dog, and the brutality of the man, over-powered by the conviction of the bystanders that he really was the hardened little wretch he was described to be; what could one poor child do? Darkness had set in; it was a low neighborhood; no help was near; resistance was useless. In another moment, he was dragged into a labyrinth of dark, narrow courts." *"What could one poor child do"* might be termed a slogan of the Dickens' child.

DICKENS' OWN CHILDHOOD

Analysts of the psychology of Dickens trace his preoccupation with neglected and rejected children to his belief that he was himself the victim of parental neglect and rejection. In a letter to [American author] Nathaniel Hawthorne he described himself as "a very small and not-overparticularly-taken-care-of-boy." Throughout his life he resented the fact that he had not been given an education. For this he blamed his father. His male parent was, he said, "as kind-hearted and generous a man as ever lived in the world." But, he added, "In the ease of his temper and the straitness of his means, he appeared to have utterly lost at this time the idea of educating me at all, and to have utterly put from him the notion that I had any claim upon him, in that regard whatever. So I degenerated into cleaning his boots of a morning, and my own; and making myself useful in the work of the little house; and looking after my younger brothers and sisters; and going on such poor errands as arose out of our poor way of living."

Dickens considered his mother rejective mainly because of an incident in his twelfth year. He had been placed to work in a blacking warehouse, a situation which filled him with humiliation and bitterness. When he was discharged as a result of a disagreement between his father and his employer, his mother intervened and induced the employer to offer to take him back. His father refused and sent the boy belatedly to school. Many years later Dickens wrote: "I never afterwards forgot, I never shall forget, I never can forget, that my mother was warm for my being sent back." In general, Dickens seemed to consider his mother as rather silly and created a caricature of her in Mrs. Nickleby, who was a rather stupid woman "who had at no time been remarkable for the possession of a very clear understanding."

Dickens also said of himself that "he always was a puny, weak youngster" prone to "violent spasmodic attacks, which used to utterly prostrate him." The active games of boys "had no charm for him, save such as lay in watching others play." Active games and sports had no charms for his young heroes either. Steerforth in *David Copperfield* is the only one who shows even a casual interest in athletic pursuits. There is little external evidence to support Dickens' picture of himself as a physically weak, rejected child, but there is no question that he had a great fund of self-pity for his lost, neglected childhood, which motivated his pleas for the rights of youth. He saw himself as a Paul Dombey who, unlike the fictional child, had survived to adulthood and he identified with many of his forlorn juvenile characters.

Identification was also responsible for a whole group of Dickens' heroines. He had a peculiar affection for a strange kind of little girl, one with a sort of saintly precocity. Agnes Wickford in *David Copperfield* was one such, as was Rose Maylie in *Oliver Twist.* Florence Dombey and Madeline Bray were others. Of Little Dorrit he said that goodness shone forth from her "pale, transparent face," and Little Nell was "a creature fresh from the hand of God." These girls were not children—they were little mothers even in their tender years. They were the embodiment of innocence—virginal, ethereal, and essentially sexless.

Most Dickensians believe that the saintly girls were based on the memory of the author's sister-in-law, Mary Hogarth, who at the age of sixteen came to live with Dickens and his wife shortly after their marriage and who died when she was seventeen. Dickens loved Mary so deeply that he wanted to share her grave. There was never a hint of the conventional (or unconventional) *ménage au trois* in his relationship with Mary, although his wife, Kate, could never live up to her husband's concept of womanhood as exemplified by her younger sister. Of Dickens' feeling for his sister-in-law, Professor Johnson, his most recent biographer, wrote: "It is impossible to exaggerate the significance of this early love and early sorrow for Dickens. His devotion to Mary was an emotion unique in his entire life, not only more enduring and unchanging than any other, but one that touched his being in a way that no other did . . . Mary set in motion in the springs of his imagination a vision of ideal womanhood that was never realized for him again.". . .

CHILDREN DYING

Numerous children die young in Dickens' novels. The first was "poor little Dick," a workhouse friend of Oliver Twist who was apparently put in the book solely to die, and on his three appearances he talks of nothing else: "I dream so much of Heaven, and angels, and kind faces that I never see when I am awake." The principal juveniles to die were Little Nell, Paul Dombey, Smike in *Nicholas Nickleby* and Dora, David Copperfield's wife. Each of these is the subject of a protracted, highly emotional deathbed scene.

Today these deathbed scenes may seem unduly dramatic and sensational: organ music with all stops out. At the time that Dickens' work was initially published they had great public appeal. Thousands of readers, particularly young girls, literally wept at the death of Little Nell. Writing of Dickens in 1858, Walter Bagehot pointed out that "The unfeeling obtuseness of the early part of this century was to be corrected by an extreme, perhaps an excessive, sensibility to human suffering in the years which have followed."

Dickens's Art Reflects His Own Life

Peter Ackroyd

Peter Ackroyd has written works of fiction, poetry, literary criticism, and biography, including a highly praised critical biography of Dickens, from which this excerpt is taken. Here he argues that Dickens's life was characterized by a surprising number of unusual features—unexpected good luck and sudden reversals of fortune—and that this pattern shaped his novels as well. For Dickens, life and literature were both subject to the same melodramatic and even incredible events. Dickens's own life was at times as strange as that of his characters, and his characters were often as eccentric as their author. Certainly, both were equally theatrical.

Ackroyd also argues that Dickens possessed a remarkable memory, so that he could not only recall scenes but recapture emotions. Having once suffered himself, he could readily empathize with the suffering of others. Thus the traumatic events of Dickens's own childhood—his father's insolvency and imprisonment—are a source of recurring themes in his novels. According to Ackroyd, these traumatic events also helped shape Dickens's sociopolitical beliefs.

Over the last one hundred and fifty years Charles Dickens has often been accused of purveying nothing but melodrama or sensationalism; his plots have been criticised for their reliance upon sudden reversals of fortune or upon the no less sudden access of wealth and happiness. Could a child like Oliver Twist really suffer such a fall from grace, at the hands of Fagin, and such an eventual redemption? Could the Dorrit family really leave the Marshalsea Prison in such an unexpected fashion? Could David Copperfield really have be-

Peter Ackroyd, *Introduction to Dickens*. London: Mandarin, 1991. Copyright © 1991 by Peter Ackroyd. Reproduced by permission.

come so renowned an author with such little apparent effort? We need only look at some of the salient facts of Dickens's own life to answer these questions.

A LIFE OF SUDDEN REVERSALS

As a small child he had been brought up in a comfortable household, in Chatham, but at the age of ten that happiness was suddenly taken away from him. He and his family moved to a house on the fringes of London, in Camden Town, and the young Dickens, who even then had hopes of becoming "a learned and distinguished man", was sent to work in a blacking factory. "No words," Dickens later wrote in a fragment of autobiography, "can express the secret agony of my soul . . . ." Then he went on to describe his sense ". . . of being utterly neglected and hopeless; of the shame I felt in my position; of the misery it was to my young heart . . ." A further catastrophe destroyed whatever happiness the family still possessed: his father, who had until then led a relatively prosperous middle-class existence as a clerk in the Naval Pay Office, was incarcerated in the Marshalsea Prison as a debtor. So it was that Dickens's childhood was torn in half.

But then, once more, everything changed. His father was suddenly freed from gaol and, a few months later, Dickens was himself released from the blacking factory. While working as a "labouring hind" all the hopes he had harboured of becoming a famous man had counted for less than nothing; but now he was enrolled in a reputable school and once more became a cheerful and vivacious child. That in itself is sufficiently remarkable a transition to justify (if not necessarily to explain) all the sudden changes of fortune which animate his fiction, but then at a later date something of momentous significance occurred; he left school and took a variety of jobs as law clerk, shorthand reporter and journalist before he realised that he could write essays or fictions which moved and delighted all those who read them. It was at the age of twenty-four, with the publication of *The Pickwick Papers*, that Charles Dickens fulfilled all of his childhood ambitions. Within a very short time, just fourteen years after he had been consigned to the darkness of a crumbling warehouse by the Thames, he became the most famous novelist in the country. When critics accused him of melodrama and sentimentality he would characteristically reply that everything he wrote was true—that these surprising reversals of fortune, these sudden conversions, were not simply the material of fiction. They represented the way of the world. Indeed for him, as we can see, they were the breath of reality itself.

SIMILAR PATTERNS IN DICKENS'S LIFE AND NOVELS

It has in the past been a matter for some speculation why Dickens, as a schoolboy and as a young man, took delight in the more sensational periodicals (like the *Terrible Register,* which he devoured as a child) and in the cheaper melodramas of the period. It has often been excused as the means by which he came into close contact with the popular culture of the period, but it was also the means by which he could confirm and strengthen that vision of the world which was vouchsafed to him as a child. It was a way of reaffirming his own unique and bewildering identity, and there is no doubt that the tone and method of these popular romances entered the spirit of his own later fiction. That in a sense is the theme of this introduction to Charles Dickens; there will be no attempt to provide a simple biography or a foreshortened exercise in literary criticism, but rather to outline the ways in which the very texture of Dickens's life affected the nature of his fiction. The "life" and the "work" are all of a piece; the shape and movement of his novels are as much a part of his being in the world as his social manner or his private behaviour, and they were directed by the same imperatives.

Two small examples may, in Dickensian fashion, set the scene. When he was courting his future wife, Catherine Hogarth, he once arrived outside the small villa in Fulham where she lived with her family—or, rather, he burst in through an open window. He was dressed in a sailor's suit and proceeded to dance a hornpipe in the middle of the drawing room where the family were sitting; he then leapt out through the window but, a few minutes later, knocked on the front door. He was wearing his usual clothes and conducted himself in an ordinary manner, making no allusion to his previous extraordinary behaviour except for a sudden "roar of laughter". A few years later he was sitting at dinner with some acquaintances when a woman turned to her husband and called him "Darling". This was not a customary endearment in the period and at once Dickens slid off his chair, lay on the floor, put one leg in the air and addressed no-one in particular with "Did she call him darling?" Then he got up from the floor, resumed his seat, and carried on as if nothing whatever had occurred.

These incidents are trivial in themselves but they do nevertheless throw an interesting light upon the procedures of Dickens's own fiction; here he has been shown to act in a dramatic and striking manner for a very brief period before resuming his customary relations with the world, like some irruption of overt theatricality in a cooler and more controlled environment. In that sense it is highly reminiscent of the way in which the more eccentric characters are displayed in his novels: they spring out with their theatrical mannerisms and verbal convolutions before subsiding once more into the background of the narrative. There is a larger point here also, since Dickens could not conceive of a character without attaching some particle of himself to its progress through the story; the more "extreme" the character, the more he was able to provide fantastic variants of his own extreme behaviour. But if Dickens's characters in certain respects resemble their creator, so that creator came also to resemble them. Dickens was changed by his novels and by the creatures who stalk through them, because in the act of creating them he came to realise more of his own possibilities; it was only while inventing Oliver Twist that he became fully aware of his own sufferings as a child, for example, and in the process of creating Ebenezer Scrooge he began to understand the springs of his own mercenary preoccupations. In order to fashion them coherently he had to become "like" them, and as a result he became more like himself.

DICKENS'S REMARKABLE MEMORY

There are other, and perhaps more easily observable, connections between the man and the novelist—perhaps the best example being the continuous presence of his extraordinary and capacious memory. He was on one occasion at a party when he became engaged in conversation with a woman who had just moved to the country; she complained of the fact that they had no neighbours, except for a certain Mr Maddison who lived a few miles distant. Some years later Dickens and the woman saw each other again at an evening party; he came towards her and said, "Well, and *how's Maddison?*" It was an extraordinary gift: well into middle age he could remember the details of his schoolfriends' lives and appearance, and this gift was itself effortlessly transplanted into his fiction. When he read to his sister the description of the grim

Mrs Pipchin from *Dombey and Son,* she exclaimed, "Good heavens! What does this mean? You have painted our lodging-house keeper and you were but two years old at the time." He was only a little older when he witnessed an incident at his family's house in Chatham when a man with a wooden leg got that appendage stuck among some small coals in the basement: the incident recurred almost fifty years later when, in Dickens's last completed novel, Silas Wegg finds ". . . his self-willed leg sticking into the ashes about half-way down". So the memory which he exercised in life was also one which helped to shape and animate his fiction.

There is another aspect of that same principle, since his friends were often astonished to note how at a first glance Dickens was able to assimilate and remember all the details of even a complicated scene. He knew as much himself and recalled on many occasions how as a child he noted and retained everything even without realising that he was doing so. It was a gift that remained with him always; it was often remarked how he could walk down a street and then afterwards remember perfectly the name of every shop as well as the nature and position of the goods which were on display in the front-windows. All this is intriguing in itself but it is, in addition, strangely reminiscent of that power of detail which fills the pages of Dickens's novels—the way in which a room,

Charles Dickens

or a character, is so completely described that it rises up in front of the reader like an hallucination. And how expertly, also, Dickens was able to maintain the appearance and characteristics of even the most minor personage for the entire length of his lengthy narratives; in later life he began to keep memoranda to assist him in the composition of his novels but, even so, the ability to maintain so large an assemblage of characters within such elaborate fictions must itself be related to those powers of recollection which he exhibited in ordinary life.

Of course that power of memory is related to his other extraordinary powers of mental organisation since, if there is one characteristic of genius, it rests in precisely that heightened use of all human faculties. Just as in life there was no neater or more disciplined person, so it seems that he was able to control and refine the more obscure aspects of his consciousness. He often compared his brain to a number of compartments, which he kept carefully labelled, and in all his activities—whether in the making of speeches, or the learning of dramatic parts—Dickens exhibited the same concentration and the same capacity for strict organisation. But memory was for him more significant than any other cognitive power, and indeed in many of his works it is seen to be the very spirit of imagination itself. In *The Haunted Man and the Ghost's Bargain,* one of the Christmas fables which he wrote after the success of *The Christmas Carol,* he ends his narrative with the sentiment, "Lord, Keep My Memory Green." For him the phrase had an acutely private application, since he always believed that it was his own memory of childhood misery and privation that opened his heart and imagination to the sufferings of others; but it had a wider reference than the wholly personal, since from that essential belief sprang Dickens's conviction that memory itself was the surest path towards imaginative sympathy and thus the act of creation itself. Memory was a form of inspiration, therefore, which linked past and present, unified humankind with the shared recollection of sorrow, and imparted to life a meaning and purpose which might not otherwise be discernible in what he once called the mere "checking off of days". The finest expression of this belief is to be found in *David Copperfield,* a novel which in a very real sense is about the nature and significance of memory, but we can see it operating throughout Dickens's life—both in his ability to recall even the most fleeting incidents of past years and in his constant preoccupation with his own childhood. The work in that sense acts as an elaborate and symbolic reenactment of the life, a purified expression of all the preoccupations which drove him forward through the world. . . .

THE CHILD WITHIN THE MAN

There are [some] respects in which that child lives on within the adult man and writer, bringing them both within the same distant perspective. Many critics have dwelt upon those occasions when the actual content of Dickens's fiction is affected by the events of his youth and infancy, for example, and indeed there are many parallels or resemblances which suggest the extent to which the traumatic incidents of his early life are constantly being replayed within his work. . . .

There are other features of his childhood, which bear a darker aspect. The boy who worked in a crumbling warehouse beside the Thames became the novelist who insistently and deliberately recorded the presence of dark and crumbling buildings which haunt his fiction like a stain. The boy whose family was incarcerated in the Marshalsea became the novelist who continually introduces into his fiction images of prisons and of prisoners. A prison appears in his first novel, *The Pickwick Papers*, where Mr Pickwick learns the meaning of suffering, and it was to emerge in his last, *The Mystery of Edwin Drood*, before the death of Dickens himself preempted an ending in which John Jasper would discover the nature of his guilt in the condemned cell. Between those novels the gaol looms everywhere—in *Nicholas Nickleby, Oliver Twist, Barnaby Rudge, The Tale of Two Cities*—and of course it reaches its apotheosis in *Little Dorrit* where the prison becomes a symbol of the human condition itself. It should not be forgotten, in this context, that as a journalist and "public man" Dickens was equally preoccupied with the theme of prisons and of prisoners—whenever he travelled to a foreign city the penitentiary was one of the first things which he wished to visit, and he never tired of discussing the nature and value of penal reform in articles and speeches. The traumatic events of his early life formed certain of his adult preoccupations, therefore, and through that connection it may be possible to find some clue to Dickens's general political and social beliefs. It would be difficult to provide a concise or coherent summary of his ideas, because those ideas were neither concise nor coherent in themselves, but this much can be said: in matters that directly touched upon the experiences of his own early life (such as the exploitation of children) he became a convincing and vociferous radical whereas, in those areas which did not so directly touch him, he characteristically adopted the stance of a conservative or moralistic disciplinarian. He took the world personally, in other words, and his most public concerns are reflections of his own private and sorrowful understanding. The point could be made another way by noting that on those occasions when he could imaginatively identify with the plight of victims, all the powerful sympathy of his nature was poured upon them; when he could not embark upon that act of identification, he became the stern man of his age. His politics and social beliefs are in that sense very much part of his own divided nature, and when claims are made for Dickens the "radical" or the "social humanitarian" it is as well to remember from what troubled origins those concerns spring.

In fact there are many aspects of his mature character which, in small matters as in large, are to be seen stretching from the shadow of his childhood. There is his extraordinary cleanliness as a man, for example, which may be related to the horror of all the dirt and (literally) blacking that surrounded him when he worked in the warehouse as a child. And then there is his wonderful neatness, which may indeed be some reflection of the disorder and even squalor which invaded his early homes; his parents were often forced to pawn items of household furniture in order to pay for their ever-increasing bills, and in that light it is possible to view with some sympathy the adult man who, on his journeys away from home, instructed his wife and relatives never to move any item of furniture from its accustomed position. He used to explain this on the grounds that he needed to visualise everything exactly as it was, but it is hard not to feel here the presence of some childhood sense of dispossession. Many biographers have of course stressed the depth and significance of that trauma, although it ought also to be emphasised that Dickens successfully and even triumphantly came through the experiences of his childhood. It would not be going too far to say, in fact, that in many important respects the strength and energy of the man were actually formed in the fire of his sufferings. Never has anyone been as persistent, as systematic, as industrious and as thorough as Charles Dickens; in addition, few writers have been as determined or as ambitious. These were precisely the qualities which saved him during his childhood tribulations, of course, and he learnt at that time a lesson he was never to forget—the world, and the human being, can be transformed by the power of the will. Always perform every task as if it were the most important thing in the world. Never *say* die. Never give up. These were the elements of his personal philosophy and, although it might not seem a very grand one, it successfully steered him through life while others clung to the wreckage of their hopes. . . .

THE END OF DICKENS'S LIFE RE-ENACTS THE BEGINNING

This in turn leads to one of the strangest aspects of Dickens's own life. For despite all his fame, and his success, there is a real possibility that at the end of his life he reverted to that solemn aspect of his own childhood; in his last years he seemed helplessly to re-enact the conditions of the first. He became sickly again; he felt himself to be unwanted and unloved; he became in many respects isolated, a man apart from his contemporaries just as the child had been apart from any companions of his own age. The vision of the world which visited him in childhood was for him the true one, and it was as if all the fame of the great English novelist had been a kind of dream from which he finally awoke to confront once more the terrors of his infancy. No doubt this is true of more people than Dickens alone, in which case some words from *A Tale of Two Cities* have more than a private import: "For, as I draw closer and closer to the end, I travel in the circle, nearer and nearer to the beginning."

CHAPTER 2

DICKENS AS A SOCIAL CRITIC

CHARLES DICKENS

Dickens's Negative Opinion of Parliament

Angus Wilson

Angus Wilson, a former librarian at the British Museum, was professor of English at the University of East Anglia, England. He wrote highly acclaimed short stories and novels as well as a study of Dickens.

In the following excerpt, Wilson argues that Dickens's firsthand observation of British Parliament in session, when he was a young parliamentary reporter, left him with an enduring contempt for this institution. Having seen the amount of time squandered on frivolous debate and bureaucratic bungling, he concluded that Parliament was both inefficient and ineffective. Yet like so many Englishmen of his generation, he was aware of the chaos, turmoil, and bloodshed resulting from the overthrow of the monarchy during the French Revolution in 1789. Moreover, having witnessed labor unrest and the Chartists' mob violence in England during his own lifetime, Dickens feared revolution and the anarchy which it unleashed as the greatest evils to befall any nation. This fear made him politically conservative, moderating his criticism of Parliament and the law. Despite their defects, he regarded them as the lesser of two evils, since they served as bulwarks against political and social chaos.

The verbiage [needless use of many words] of Parliamentary proceedings, transferred to other settings, is facetiously [jokingly] imitated, I suppose, in the proceedings of the Pickwick Club [in Dickens's novel *Pickwick Papers*] and the very unfunny, irrelevant second chapter of *Nicholas Nickleby*, where we are given an account of a meeting of the United Metropolitan Improved Hot Muffin and Crumpet Baking and Punc-

Angus Wilson, *The World of Charles Dickens*. London: Martin Secker and Warburg, 1970. Copyright © 1970 by Angus Wilson. Reproduced by permission.

tual Delivery Company. The impression made upon [Dickens] by elections gives us the Eatanswill chapter of *Pickwick Papers*, whilst the contempt of the M.P. [Member of Parliament] for his electors once the election is over is satirized in Mr Gregsbury's dismissal of the deputation in *Nicholas Nickleby*. But these are very early novels, and all he had seen from the reporter's gallery of the House of Commons or at the hustings soon vanished from his world, although M.P.s and their jockeying remain a feature of his satire.

His only picture of Parliament in session is historical and seen from outside the closed doors of the Chamber. The description in *Barnaby Rudge* (1841) of the presentation to the Commons of the Protestant petition by Lord George Gordon and his mob of followers is masterly—one of the many beautifully organized and controlled crowd scenes which punctuate this mob-enthralled novel against mobs. But it is to be noted that Dickens's fictional interest in Parliament as a bulwark against the Protestant mob of 1780 came, not from any tender memory for the Parliament he had watched in action for four years, but from his alarm at the physical force element in Chartism [labor movement demanding parliamentary reforms for workers] and the violent rising of Chartists in the provinces in the four or five years before the publication of his fine historical novel. Lord George Gordon's bogus and dangerous petition must have spoken to all good, law-abiding readers of *Barnaby Rudge* as another, earlier version of the wicked Charter [petition for rights presented by workers]. Even so it is notable that the Commons themselves do little to control the mob in the novel; this is done by the bravery of an individual member, a military man, General Conway.

Dickens: A Radical Liberal

The historical example he chose fitted well among his own prejudices. I do not mean to imply that Dickens would have substituted iron rule for democracy. The idea sometimes put about of him as a "crypto-Fascist" [secret sympathizer with Fascism] is, as I hope my picture of him will show, a false sophistication. But when it came to Parliament, his radical liberalism had a strong emphasis on the radical. In his chapter on his hero, [Puritan and anti-royalist leader in the seventeenth-century English Civil War, Oliver] Cromwell, in his *Child's History of England* he writes: "As that Parliament did not please him either, and would not proceed to the business of the country, he jumped into a coach one morning, took six guards with him, and sent them to the right-about. I wish this had been a warning to Parliaments to avoid long speeches, and do more work." This, of course, is the tone of much reporting from Parliament that we get in the newspapers today. It is the natural reaction of those who have to listen to public debates with their intermixture of so much party propaganda talk, and so much seemingly facetiously schoolboy "House of Commons is the best club in London" wit; it is the natural reaction of those who never see the real work of Members of Parliament in committee or in constituency business. In his letters Dickens sometimes expressed grave concern for the failure of the working of the Parliamentary system; but in the fictional world this concern becomes translated into the once-for-all ironic contempt of the famous opening of the fortieth chapter of *Bleak House* (1852–3): "England has been in a dreadful state for some weeks, Lord Coodle would go out, Sir Thomas Doodle wouldn't come in, and there being nobody in Great Britain (to speak of) except Coodle and Doodle, there had been no Government." So much for Parliament and the party system, those bastions of the mid-Victorian constitution.

Added to his contempt for the Law, his contempt for Parliament should have made him some sort of a revolutionary, whether of left or right (as we should say now). It is indeed just what "mature", "responsible" men—Members of Parliament, Cabinet ministers, Q.C.s [Queen's Council, a lawyer who conducts a court case], and judges—would expect from a man whose opinion of two of the great bastions of England's society had been formed in youth from menial, irresponsible positions (or, at the best, with his reporting, purely as a spectator). It is not from office boys and clerks, or even from reporters, that mature, responsible men expect mature, responsible judgements. And in one sense they are right. For men of standing in the world of affairs, the institutions they serve are alive only in the work they execute. Of this work in any detail there is no trace in Dickens's novels.

YET NOT A REVOLUTIONARY

Many reasons are given why Charles Dickens could not carry his contempt for the status quo into a revolutionary logic—the fear of anarchy of a self-made man with genteel, even snobbish frame of temper is one. But it is easy to make too much of this. Dickens earned good money, lived well, brought up his children comfortably, liked to mix with notable people. This is true. But as he came to be a world fig-

---

THE SOCIAL-PROBLEM NOVEL

Several nineteenth-century writers—among them Charles Dickens, George Eliot, and Elizabeth Gaskell— wrote works that can be termed "social-problem novels." These novels not only focus on social issues and economic conditions but may have far-reaching political implications. This type of novel is essentially didactic: its aim is to educate its readers by exposing the various conditions which threaten to endanger the stability of society. This point is made by Josephine M. Guy, lecturer in English at the University of Nottingham and author of several studies of British literature.

The terms "social-problem" or "industrial" novel are generally used to refer to a body of English fiction written in the late 1840s and 1850s which allegedly takes as its subject-matter large-scale problems in contemporary British society, problems which in turn were the product of changing demographic patterns and changes in work practices associated with the accelerating industrialization of the British economy. This literary engagement with contemporary affairs in turn depended upon what was claimed to be a new kind of relationship between the novel and the social and political worlds which produced it. Social-problem novels are typically distinguished from earlier novels, and from other works contemporary with them, by their attempt to comment on, and stimulate debate about, matters of general public and political concern. Thomas Carlyle's portmanteau phrase, the "Condition-of-England question", is often used to describe these social matters; they centre on the perception that social order was under threat from conflicts between various interest groups in society, and particularly from the discontent of the increasingly impoverished and degraded working classes. The intentions of the writers who address these issues are assumed to be both serious and, more importantly, political. So social-problem novelists are commonly credited with the intention of trying to educate, and therefore by implication to change, the opinions and prejudices of their readers. In so doing, they are seen to be implying that the novel can, and should, have an important role to play in social and political life.

Josephine M. Guy, *The Victorian Social-Problem Novel: The Market, the Individual and Communal Life.* Houndmills, UK: Macmillan, 1996, pp. 3–4.

ure, he outgrew most of the snobbery which had inevitably attached to him when he was making his way. By 1860 when he wrote *Great Expectations* he scorned gentility as fully and deeply as any hater of the social system could ask. Yet he continued always to fear deeply the overthrow of settled order. Profound disenchantment with social institutions, anxiety about any sort of social upheaval, go constantly together in his career. It is often explained by saying that he feared mobs. No doubt he did. This is sometimes said with a certain air of criticism by people who themselves would greatly fear a mob if they ever met one. And it really explains nothing. Coming from a small bourgeois family, born not twenty years after the Terror of the French Revolution, it is much more astonishing that he should espouse the popular cause at all than that he should fear its violent consequences. Yet throughout his career, and notably in *A Tale of Two Cities*, however much he warned against popular violence, he always insisted that the eighteenth-century French aristocracy had only reaped the harvest that they had sown.

The cause of his deep fear of social upheaval, which marries at times so oddly with his contempt for the social system, lies, I think, in two very differing aspects of his view of life. The first is his very real belief in evil, of which we shall see much more when we come to his great novels. But a deep-seated belief in evil, especially in evil evidenced in violence, hardly allows for social revolution. No promise of Utopia can be worth the risk of evil unleashed, that a violent revolution offers. Sympathetic though he was to the grievances of the Chartists, "it is unnecessary for us to observe that we have not the least sympathy with physical force Chartism in the abstract," he wrote in the *Examiner* in 1848, "or with tried and convicted Physical Force Chartists in particular. Apart from the atrocious designs to which these men, beyond all question, willingly and easily subscribed . . . they have done too much damage to the cause of rational liberty and freedom all over the world to be regarded in any other light than as enemies of the common weal [welfare, prosperity], and the worst foes of the common people." Evil in action was for Dickens a fearsome reality—the beast unleashed.

The second was the opposite—an enjoyment of the richness and variety of life even at his most despairing moments. Dickens was not without certain puritanisms; he shared some of the prudery of his time; but he was as constant an advocate of play as he was of work. Play, enjoyment, variety, above all absurdity in variety—these are the very core of the world of Dickens. For all his radicalism, for all his deep concern to combat individual social evils, his comic sense made him—like most satirists—far more conservative than either his intellect or even his emotions often allowed him to recognize. To say all this, that his sense of evil and his sense of comedy prevented him from translating his sourness and his despair into a logical system of rejection of society, is only to say that, whatever his inclinations, thoughts and feelings, he instinctively recognized the sources of his art—the crude but powerful dramatic analysis of evil, the subtle, pervasive poetry of comic absurdity. In that scheme the Law stood, however weakly, as some negative check against ill-doing, and was an absurdity rich in comic potential. As to Parliament, it was as Law, though less important.

Dickens Condemns Victorian Public Education

Philip Collins

Dickens's social criticism manifested itself, among other things, in his active support of educational reform—both as a means of improving the lives of the lower classes and as a means of preventing crime. Interested as he was in pedagogic theory, methodology, and practice, he visited various types of schools in England (and in America, on his visits there) in order to evaluate them pragmatically. Dickens was not particularly concerned with the private schools for children of the affluent or privileged classes. Instead he focused his attention on those schools which educated society's less fortunate, including those schools attached to workhouses (charitable institutions for the orphaned and the destitute). The following report, detailing Dickens's opinion of charity and workhouse schools, was written by Philip Collins, professor of English at the University of Leicester and author of several books on Dickens.

Charity Schools varied, . . . but Dickens's indictment of them, both for their inefficiency and for the humiliation they imposed upon their pupils, can be substantiated from the reports of many educational commentators of the age. What Dickens wanted, he had seen in America in 1842—the Boston Blind School, for instance, where there were "no charity uniforms, no wearisome repetition of the same dull ugly dress"; every child was dressed after his own taste, and his individuality was kept "distinct and unimpaired." This school also evoked Dickens's comment that "a Public Charity is immeasurably better than a Private Foundation, no matter how munificently . . . endowed", for the State can thus appear as the kind protector instead of the stern master of the poor. In Britain, too, he knew some good Charity Schools, though these were generally a cut above those in the novels: they were schools established, not by the rich for the poor, but by members of a middle-class trade for the "orphan and necessitous children" of their brethren. Though they appealed for donations, they were examples of self-help, since only subscribers' children were eligible; thus they avoided the taint of patronage which Dickens always hated. He particularly admired the Commercial Travellers' School; it was one of his favourite charities, and he gave two splendid speeches on its behalf, one of them describing a visit there (the children had "an excellent way of looking those in authority full in the face"—this was one of the many features he approved). Before becoming a novelist, he had reported on another such school, where there was "no degrading dress—no charity livery to remind the children of their destitution, or their patrons of their munificence." And on a visit to the Stepney Red Coat and Green Coat schools in 1838 he expressed pleasure at what he saw, "'Charity' schools though they were." But it is characteristic that none of these better Charity Schools get into the novels.

THE WORKHOUSE SCHOOL

The workhouse school . . . came even lower than the Charity School in social esteem, and Dickens, who so often attacked the New Poor Law, had something to say about them, though not in his novels. Oliver Twist's "education" was hardly scholastic. "Well!", said one of the Guardians, "You have come here to be educated, and taught a useful trade."—"So", said the other, "you'll begin to pick oakum [loose fiber obtained from picking old ropes to pieces; often task of paupers and convicts in England] tomorrow morning at six o'clock." But one of his first contributions to *Household Words* was "A Walk in a Workhouse." Though he saw much to commend, he was oppressed by the general air of lassitude and hopelessness, of stern discipline and poor feeding. The paupers' faces were correspondingly "depressed and subdued, and wanted colour", but fortunately the children fared better. Dickens visited their schools, pleased to find the infants well fed and uncowed by strangers ("And it was comfortable to see two mangy pauper rocking-horses rampant in a corner"), noting the girls' cheerful healthy appearance, and the large airy yard where the boys roamed unrestrained. Characteristically and, in the circumstances, sensibly, he was more concerned with the schools' tone than their educational quality. His one remark on the scholastic activities was that the boys had been drawing large ships upon the schoolroom wall: he approved, but wished that, in addition, their playground had contained "a mast with shrouds and stays set up for practice (as they have in the Middlesex House of Correction)." He often expressed delight in this favourite piece of equipment for boys' institutions: here, he introduced the reference to make his familiar point, that prisons were often more comfortable and better equipped than workhouses, or indeed the ordinary dwellings of the poor. "Do they teach trades in workhouses, and try to fit *their* people (the worst part of them) for Society?" he wrote, when arguing that prison-reform had a low priority among expensive social needs. "Come with me to Tothill Fields Bridewell, . . . and I will show you what a workhouse girl is. Or look to my Walk in a Workhouse. . . ."

A Good Example

What a workhouse and its school should be, appeared in his account of the South Boston House of Industry: "very plain and simple, as it ought to be, but arranged with a view to peace and comfort." There, instead of living in "great, long, rambling wards, where a certain amount of weazen [wizened; shrivelled or dried up in appearance] life may mope, and pine, and shiver, all day long", the paupers had decent little individual rooms, thus acquiring "a motive for exertion and becoming pride." The pauper children lived in a pretty little school, with miniature furniture and Lilliputian [reduced in size] stairs, under arrangements entirely "excellent and gentle." Dickens departed "with a lighter heart than ever I have taken leave of pauper infants yet." Their plight was indeed generally wretched; as an Assistant Commissioner told the Newcastle Commission, "I know nothing more pathetic than a Workhouse School."

Many further articles on workhouses appeared in his periodicals, often discussing the problems of their schools. As one contributor remarked, the Union atmosphere inevitably harmed the children who grew up in it. Courage and enterprise were squeezed out of them, and "the utter dulness that begets a hopeless manhood takes the vacant space." Moreover, most workhouse schools were inefficient and heartless, largely because their teachers were ill-paid and badly regulated. Kay-Shuttleworth's great remedy was to remove the children into special residential District Pauper Schools or into Union day-schools some distance from the workhouse itself: Dickens and his contributors supported this plan, *Household Words* containing eulogies of outstanding District Schools such as Norwood. Later, some doubts about this system were expressed: it would be better still for children to enjoy a normal family life, and education in an ordinary local school. One of Dickens's contributors, advocating such a boarding-out system, stressed that the administrative machinery for supervising it had improved since the days of Mr. Bumble and Mr. Sowerberry: "Having some authority to speak in the name of Oliver Twist, we here record on his behalf . . . that it was his misfortune to be a pauper child in days when pauper children were out of sight and out of mind. The light has been let in upon them since." Another constant theme in these workhouse articles is the importance of giving pauper children sound "industrial" [vocational] training: the boys should learn farming or a trade, and the girls, growing up without the domestic training they would get in a family, should learn cooking and other skills. Dickens always wanted education to be practical and "useful", especially when the children's parentage was such that they were likely to become paupers or criminals unless they could start life knowing an honest trade.

THE SHORT-TIME SYSTEM

Many of these concerns recur in an article Dickens wrote about the Limehouse School of Industry, run by the "earnest and humane" Guardians of the Stepney Union. It was not his first visit: "these have long been excellent schools," he wrote; ". . . I first saw them twelve or fifteen years ago." He had returned to see how they operated the new Half-time or Short-time system, and he was well pleased. "I have never visited any similar establishment with so much pleasure," he wrote in the Visitors' Book. "I have never seen any so well administered, and I have never seen children more reasonably, humanely, and intelligently treated." This opinion, reiterated in his published account, greatly encouraged the local Guardians for many years thereafter, we are told. It was indeed a vigorous and enthusiastic article. . . .

The Short-time system seen in operation here received Dickens's emphatic approval. The pupils not only learned more in eighteen hours a week at their books than in thirty-six, but were also "far quicker and brighter than of yore"; and the teaching-costs were correspondingly reduced. Here for once, Dickens was following instead of giving a lead to his journalistic colleagues. Three earlier articles in *All the Year Round* had advocated this Half-time system, the last of them hailing as "a proved fact" this wonderful discovery that halving the school hours improved their pupils' education, while also at a stroke doubling the capacity of schools and the child-load of teachers. "To this, we shall all come some of these days," the article concluded, urging that the system be immediately applied to the schooling of poor children, whose parents would more willingly leave them at school if they could simultaneously hold a half-time job. Dickens was impressed by this enthusiastic advocacy of a panacea so timely and economical, but it is typical that he went to see for himself one of the schools well-known for its adoption of the system: also, that he prepared himself by reading a "small bundle of papers" on the idea. His essay is typical in two other ways: first, that it starts with an indignant passage about the "shameful instances of neglect of children" visible on every London street, and a demand that the State should "with a strong hand take them while they are yet children, and wisely train them"; second, that when approaching his theme of the Half-time system Dickens begins by recalling his own schooldays, how always "our attention began to wander when we had pored over our books for some hours."

At least the workhouse child received some education, and it could be a good one. Even the juvenile delinquent in prison went to school: Dickens describes the boys at their lessons in Newgate—"fourteen such terrible little faces we never beheld." But there were some children who never enjoyed even this fleeting acquaintance with a schoolroom.

The Historical Context of *Bleak House*

Graham Storey

Bleak House is widely regarded as both a literary masterpiece and a remarkable exposé of various aspects of Dickens's England. In this novel, according to Graham Storey, Dickens presents some of the most controversial issues—legal, religious, political, and socioeconomic—in Victorian society. The one dominating the novel is the corruption of the High Court of Chancery, which had become a national scandal. Another major source of dissension alluded to in the work was the attempt by some members of the Anglican Church, the Church of England, to restore to the faith its original Catholic rites and dogma (even though it had broken with Rome in the sixteenth century, during the reign of Henry VIII). Yet another topical issue in the work was the arrogant assumption by members of the aristocracy that only they had the right to govern the country, an assumption increasingly disputed by the working class and a growing middle class. No less shocking were the appalling conditions of the London slums, a festering sore in the city and a source of filth and disease. Juxtaposed to the poverty and degradation of the slums was the contentious issue of "telescopic philanthropy"—that is, charity which directed its efforts to projects overseas while ignoring the London poor and needy.

These five points depicted in the novel and mirroring contemporary topical issues in Victorian England, are analyzed by Storey, Reader in English at Cambridge University, in his critical study of *Bleak House.*

As John Butt and Kathleen Tillotson showed many years ago, in *Dickens at Work* (1957), *Bleak House* is a remarkably topical novel. No less than five of the major targets of its anger, as they show in detail, were public issues in 1851, the year in which Dickens began to write it: the abuses of the court of Chancery; the establishment the year before of the Roman Catholic hierarchy in England; political misgovernment (for a period, no government at all); the London slums; and what Dickens calls "Telescopic philanthropy", the ignoring of social needs at home for the spurious excitement of sending out missions abroad.

It is true that neither the appalling conditions of the London poor nor the abuses of Chancery were new subjects for Dickens. Jacob's Island in *Oliver Twist* is the first of his London slums; Want and Ignorance are the children who, in a vision, convert Scrooge in *A Christmas Carol*, his first Christmas book; a long passage in *Dombey and Son* cries out against the horrifying effects of bad sanitation. The most serious and pathetic point (as Dickens described it in a letter of December 1852) that he had tried to make in *Pickwick* was the lingering death of a Chancery prisoner. What makes *Bleak House* a landmark, the first of Dickens's "dark period" novels, is that, for the first time, he has created a whole world out of such and similar evils. It is the whole of contemporary society that he anatomizes. Of his peculiar gift for seeing connexions between things not glimpsed by most people he was fully aware: "I think", he wrote to his friend Lord [Edward Bulwer] Lytton in 1865, with a touch of irony, "it is my infirmity to fancy or perceive relations in things which are not apparent generally."

These five major issues, then, constitute the true historical background to *Bleak House.* Together they form what Thomas Carlyle, the most powerful intellectual influence on Dickens, had called, in *Chartism* (1840), the "Condition-of-England question", and, more vehemently in *Past and Present* (1843), where he analyses the consequences of failing to solve it, "universal social gangrene". To understand the novel's impact on its first readers we must grasp the immediacy of each of these issues and the precision—and intensity—with which Dickens deals with them. In a novel pervaded by irony, the title *Bleak House* itself is surely a parody of the major English event of 1851, the Great Exhibition [public display of works of art, industry]: the grim reality beneath the materialistic complacency, the boasted "commerce of all nations."

CHANCERY

The opening chapter, "In Chancery", brilliantly suggests the novel's universal blight; its centre, the case of Jarndyce and Jarndyce, being heard, as it has been for many years, by the Lord Chancellor in the High Court of Chancery, was highly topical too. Chancery abuse had been a target for reformers for several decades; but in 1851 it had become a major national issue. "Trickery, evasion, procrastination, spoliation, botheration . . . false pretences of all sorts . . . Shirking and sharking, in all their many varieties", as John Jarndyce puts it, are the fruits of Jarndyce and Jarndyce; almost all had been anticipated in leading anti-Chancery articles in *The Times* during 1851.

Jarndyce and Jarndyce was itself based on a notorious Chancery case, begun in 1834 and still proceeding; a similar case in Staffordshire was the model for what drove Gridley all but mad. National demands procured some reform in an Act of August 1851; for Dickens only the burning away of the Court "in a great funeral pyre" could accomplish what he wanted and in his way achieved in "Chancellor" Krook's spontaneous combustion.

But the language of the final paragraph describing Krook's death (ch. 32: "The Appointed Time") goes far beyond legal reform:

> [Krook] has died the death of all Lord Chancellors in all Courts, and of all authorities in all places under all names soever, where false pretences are made, and where injustice is done.

In *Past and Present*, Carlyle had painted the treatment and despair of a disappointed Chancery client as an example of general administrative futility. Dickens has gone further in both directions: he has made the most of the topical appeal of Chancery abuse to his readers; he has also made of it a symbol of universal corruption.

A RELIGIOUS CRISIS

Even more widely discussed than Chancery abuse in 1851 was the religious crisis caused by the establishment of the Roman Catholic hierarchy in England the year before— freely referred to as "Papal Aggression." For Dickens, who hated the Roman Catholic Church, the Oxford Movement, the party within the Anglican Church that aimed to restore it to its primitive [original] "Catholic" roots, and in particular E.B. Pusey, its new Oxford leader (the "Pusey and Newman Corporation", as Carlyle called it in a letter), were directly responsible; and they were deeply distasteful to him. In *Bleak House* he derides them. Mrs Pardiggle is not only distinguished for her "rapacious benevolence", but is clearly a Puseyite as well: her five sons are named after saints and heroes of the primitive [Catholic] Church; they are taken to Matins "(very prettily done)" at 6.30 A.M. all the year round; and the little book she gives to the brickmakers is no doubt a Puseyite Tract ("It's a book fit for a babby [baby], and I'm

THE FOG IN *BLEAK HOUSE*

American scholar Edmund Wilson, one of the most eminent literary critics of the twentieth century, was the author of numerous highly praised studies of literature and culture. His long essay on Dickens, from which this excerpt is taken, was published more than fifty years ago and has become a classic.

In his analysis of Bleak House, *Wilson pays close attention to the language and imagery used by Dickens at the beginning of the novel to describe the fog enveloping the city of London and the Court of Chancery. The fog, argues Wilson, provides a crucial key to interpreting the major themes of the novel.*

Bleak House begins in the London fog, and the whole book is permeated with fog and rain. . . .

In *Bleak House* the fog stands for Chancery, and Chancery stands for the whole web of clotted antiquated institutions in which England stifles and decays. All the principal elements in the story—the young people, the proud Lady Dedlock, the philanthropic gentleman John Jarndyce, and Tom-all-Alone's, the rotting London slum—are involved in the exasperating Chancery suit, which, with the fog-bank of precedent looming behind it, . . . obscures and impedes at every point the attempts of men and women to live natural lives. Old Krook, with his legal junkshop, is Dickens' symbol for the Lord Chancellor himself; the cat that sits on his shoulder watches like the Chancery lawyers the caged birds in Miss Flite's lodging; Krook's death by spontaneous combustion is Dickens' prophecy of the fate of Chancery and all that it represents.

Edmund Wilson, "The Two Scrooges," in *The Wound and the Bow: Seven Studies in Literature.* Rev. ed. London: W.H. Allen, 1952, pp. 33–34.

not a babby", says one of them). The ladies who want
Jarndyce's money to house "the Sisterhood of Medieval
Marys" are clearly Puseyites too. But the most dangerous
ones—equally derided—are the fashionable guests at Chesney Wold [an aristocratic house] who have set up a Dandyism [being overly concerned with superficial appearances,
e.g. with religious rites] in Religion. . . .

AN EFFETE ARISTOCRACY

There is yet another "Dandyism" [here meaning a smug
sense of superiority] among the guests at Chesney Wold: the
conviction of "the brilliant and distinguished circle" that, in
the choice of a Party to govern the country, "nobody is in
question but Boodle and his retinue and Buffy and *his* retinue. These are the great actors for whom the stage is reserved" (ch. 12). "A People" there may be—but they are only
stage extras; it is Boodle and Buffy who are "the born first-
actors, managers and leaders, and no others can appear
upon the scene for ever and ever." This belief of a few aristocratic families in their sacred right to govern the country—
and to exclude all others, however able—was highly topical
too. In February 1851, after Lord John Russell's administration was defeated, there was literally a two weeks' hiatus
[break or recess] in government; and one reason was the
Party leaders' belief that no one else could be brought in for
the task. Dickens's sarcasm echoes similar attacks in *The
Times;* and he begins ch. 40 ("National and Domestic") even
more pointedly:

> England has been in a dreadful state for some weeks. Lord
> Coodle would go out, Sir Thomas Doodle wouldn't come in,
> and there being nobody in Great Britain (to speak of) except
> Coodle and Doodle, there has been no Government.

The first readers of *Bleak House* would certainly have re-
sponded to the topicality of this; just as they would have
done to Volumnia Dedlock's unfortunate mistake in asking
Sir Leicester what the Party's "enormous expense" in winning had been for. Bribery was still an integral part of every
election. . . .

THE LONDON SLUMS

The filth, hideous overcrowding and lack of sanitation of the
slums are a major part of the bleakness of *Bleak House.*
Tom-all-Alone's (described in all its foulness in both chs. 16

and 46) is the most horrible: it appears, in fact, in all of the titles for the novel considered by Dickens before settling on *Bleak House*. The brickmakers' hovels near St. Alban's, with their wretched and mostly drunken inhabitants, are nearly as bad. And they are reinforced by another source of evil, the rat-infested paupers' graveyard, where Captain Hawdon and Jo are both buried and Lady Dedlock dies. This was founded on fact too. It was the notorious graveyard of St. Martin's-in-the-Fields, which Dickens had known as a boy. Dickens brings all these disease-bearing pollutions, and others, together—appropriately—on the night of Krook's death:

> It is a fine steaming night to turn the slaughterhouses, the unwholesome trades, the sewage, bad water, and burial-grounds to account, and give the Registrar of Deaths some extra business. (ch. 32)

Overcrowding, bad drainage, contaminated water—and the diseases they engender—were, again, highly topical issues in 1851; made worse, in many people's eyes, by the proximity and prosperity of the Great Exhibition. Dickens had attacked them as early as his terrible picture of Jacob's Island in *Oliver Twist*. He attacked them again, with the crimes they led to, in a long passage in *Dombey and Son* (ch. 17). From 1849 onwards, sanitary reform was a major subject of his public speeches and journalism: "the most momentous of all earthly questions", he called it in his address "To Working Men", published in *Household Words* on 7 October 1854. Cholera epidemics made it more urgent; his brother-in-law Henry Austin's work as Secretary of the General Board of Health, and the copies of the reports Austin sent him, helped to make him highly informed on the appalling problems involved. *Bleak House* not only gives hideous examples of slums and pauper graveyards; it shows how they contaminate high and low alike; that disease is no respecter of class.

Dickens gave the same grim warning in a speech at the Metropolitan Sanitary Association dinner in May 1851. In *Bleak House*, Jo's infection of Esther with smallpox shows it dramatically come true. We are not allowed to forget the cholera, either: Guster, the Snagsbys' epileptic servant, is a survivor of the 1849 Tooting "baby-farm" scandal, in which 180 pauper children died from cholera and neglect (Dickens devoted four articles in the *Examiner* to exposing it). In a new Preface to *Oliver Twist*, of 1850, Dickens had written of the necessity to improve slum conditions:

> I have always been convinced that this reform must precede
> all other Social Reforms; that it must prepare the way for Ed-
> ucation, even for Religion; and that, without it, those classes
> of the people which increase the fastest must become so des-
> perate, and be made so miserable, as to bear within them-
> selves the certain seeds of ruin to the whole community.

The bearing of those seeds, principally by Jo, is brilliantly
and horribly shown in *Bleak House.*

MISPLACED CHARITY

The last of the novel's major topical issues was what Dickens sarcastically calls "Telescopic philanthropy", misguided
benevolence abroad, which ignored the acute social problems at home. It is yet another form of blindness, seen at its
most extreme and absurd in the novel's two famous "philan-
thropists", Mrs Jellyby and Mrs Pardiggle. Mrs Jellyby's eyes
"had a curious habit of seeming to look a long way off. As if
. . . they could see nothing nearer than Africa!" Mrs Pardiggle lavishes her family's contributions on her Tockahoopo
Indians; but is utterly blind to the realities of the brickmakers' wretched lives. Jo, the destitute crossing-sweeper, sitting on the doorstep of the Society for the Propagation of the
Gospel in Foreign Parts, munching "his dirty bit of bread",
makes the point even more emphatically; as does the appalling picture of his ignorance, when questioned by the
Coroner at the inquest on Nemo (ch. 11). We know that this
was modelled on fact, on the case of a boy named George
Ruby, about fourteen years old, called, on 8 January 1850, at
the Guildhall, to give evidence in a case of assault. Jo's answers to the Coroner are remarkably similar to the boy's,
given in a report in Dickens's own *Household Narrative.*

Mrs Jellyby may have had her prototype in Mrs Caroline
Chisholm, whose Family Colonization Loan Society for helping emigrants to Australia Dickens in fact supported, yet
whose housekeeping and dirty-faced children . . . haunted
his dreams. But, much more than that, she is a representative of Exeter Hall, the centre of evangelical missionary activity in London, for which Dickens, like Carlyle, had a profound contempt. Her African project, to educate the natives of
Borrioboola-Gha, "on the left bank of the Niger", echoes almost exactly a disastrous expedition to the River Niger in
1841, to abolish the slave trade and to improve agriculture.

Dickens had reviewed the published account of it in the *Examiner* of 19 August 1848, and had duly made the point about Exeter Hall, which had, of course, been "hot in its behalf":

> It might be laid down as a very good general rule of social and political guidance, that whatever Exeter Hall champions, is the thing by no means to be done.

The Niger expedition was a fiasco: those who survived fever were murdered by "King Boy"; "King Obi" returned to selling slaves. Mrs. Jellyby's project was a similar disaster, "the King of Borrioboola wanting to sell everybody—who survived the climate—for Rum."

The moral was clear: charity, desperately needed, must begin at home.

Dickens as Social Reformer

Ivor Brown

Ivor Brown, scholar, drama critic, and former editor of *The Observer*, has written numerous books, including several studies of Shakespeare and the highly praised *Dickens in His Time*. This excerpt is taken from an article by Brown specially written for a collection of essays published on the centenary of Dickens's death. The article traces Dickens's attitude to the evils of his day and surveys various aspects of Victorian society that were modified or reformed by parliamentary legislation enacted during his lifetime.

Brown shows that, as a social reformer, Dickens's assumption was that laws had to be formulated with "decency" and "generosity." These are terms not generally used in political discourse but rather terms intended to appeal to the public's conscience, as Dickens deliberately did in his essays and novels. Although Dickens was disillusioned with parliamentary reform, he disliked the tyranny of trade unions and was adamantly opposed to the violent overthrow of the government.

In his discussion of Dickens's life and fiction, Brown initially analyzes Dickens's criticism of the prison system. He turns next to Dickens's comments on the workhouse, an institution established by Parliament in the Poor Law of 1834 and scathingly condemned by Dickens in *Oliver Twist*. In *The Old Curiosity Shop* and, above all, in *Hard Times*, Dickens focused his attention on the mills and factories which were supposed to have been regulated by the Factory Act of 1833 but which still continued to exploit child labor, employing boys from the age of nine for a workday of twelve hours, excluding meal breaks.

Thus even though Dickens was impatient with the

Ivor Brown, "Dickens as Social Reformer," *Charles Dickens 1812–1870: A Centenary Volume*, edited by E.W.F. Tomlin. London: Weidenfeld and Nicolson, 1969. Copyright © 1969 by George Weidenfeld and Nicolson Limited. Reproduced by permission.

slow pace of parliamentary reform, Brown points
out that he found no viable alternative: not until
fourteen years after his death did the middle-class
socialists begin to work on a drastic reform of the
Poor Law. As Brown argues, Dickens's works provided the impetus for reform—what he terms "the
raw material of social progress." But it was left to
others to complete the process.

Reformers are of two kinds. There are the writers and
speakers who expose evils and rouse public indignation.
They create what is frequently called the climate of opinion
and may put thunder in the air. Dickens excelled in his
power to illuminate a scandal with his lightning flash of
phrase amid the anger of his indignation. In this kind of agitation he was as much "the Inimitable" [beyond compare]
as he was in his tumultuous presentation of the human comedy. His attacks on the callousness and corruption of the Victorian ruling class and its officials were sometimes so
scathing as to embarrass those on his side who were trying
to achieve social improvements by legal and administrative
methods. They inevitably had to make use of stupid people
and slow Parliamentary methods. It was necessary to practise some sufferance of dolts and even knaves. They had to
collaborate with patience while Dickens used his freedom to
castigate without stint.

There is the second type of reformer whose work is less
spectacular but none the less essential. Collecting detailed
evidence of scandalous conditions and drafting reports and
new laws is not exciting; but it has to be done. For this kind
of work Dickens was suited neither by occupation nor by inclination. He was too busy as a novelist, journalist, editor,
letter-writer, and public speaker to apply himself to the
drudgery of formulating clause by clause reformist pro-
grammes and measures, attending committees, and lobby-
ing for support amid public apathy and discouragement,
Parliamentary sloth, and factious opposition. He was several
times invited to stand for a seat in the House of Commons
and properly refused to do so. That was not his line and we
may be thankful that he rejected all such approaches. If he
had been harnessed to the team of Radical members and
forced to listen to long debates, English literature would

have been disastrously deprived. He drove ahead with his fiction based on fact while others planned and contrived to alter the facts. It was a fair division of labour. He knew his part and played it superbly.

VEHICLES OF REFORM

There are various paths open to the critic of a cruel and unjust society. He can advocate violent overthrow of the existing régime, as did some of the Chartists. He can work through the constitutional means of legislation and Parliamentary action. He can turn to the other implements of power such as the trade unions. But to all these methods he was unsympathetic and sometimes actually hostile. Violence he loathed. His terrifying descriptions of raging mobs were not limited to the fury of the French in *A Tale of Two Cities*. His strictures in *The Old Curiosity Shop* on an English riot in the Midlands is ample proof of his social pacifism. Amid the screams of orphans and widows, Little Nell saw "maddened men, armed with sword and fire-brand," rushing through streets full of rumbling coffins "on errands of destruction to work no ruin so surely as their own." If that was the product of Chartism's fanatical fringe, Dickens foresaw not an England reformed but an England smouldering in the flames of an inferno.

Of Parliament he was contemptuous. In 1846, when certain important improvements were being achieved, he wrote of "The Great Dust Heap down at Westminster." He may have had Mr Boffin's repulsive mounds of refuse and ordure already in mind when he used this image. That was no way in which to make allies and promote causes in the House of Commons where Ashley Cooper, who became the Earl of Shaftesbury in 1851, was steadily and splendidly at work. It was largely through the labours of that devoted man in the "Dust Heap" that the hours of work in mines, mills, and factories were limited. His Lodging House Act of 1851, a measure of housing reform, was described by Dickens as the best piece of legislation that ever came from Parliament. Yet Dickens continued to deride the members of both Houses as snobs, sloths, jobbers and wastrel dandies. There were many such, but sweeping generalizations were unjust and tactless. There were some victories even at despised Westminster.

Dickens was far from approving of the old Combination Laws and naturally resented the persecution of trade unionists which continued when combination had been legalized. In 1834 there had been the conviction and transportation [sending criminals overseas to penal colony] of six farm-labourers at Tolpuddle in Dorset for modest and innocent trade union activities. But in *Hard Times* there is more ha-tred of trade union tyranny than appreciation of what in-dustrial organization could beneficially effect. His investiga-tion of Lancashire, its staple industry, and the strike of the textile workers in 1854 has been criticized as hasty and su-perficial. Certainly it left him in two minds. He was of course sympathetic to the over-worked and under-paid men and women in the mills, but he despised the wind-bag Slack-bridge as much as he loathed Gradgrind and Bounderby. He could see no future in singing "England, Arise" if the prole-tarian choir were led by frothy, self-seeking rabble-rousers of the Slackbridge kind while independent men like Stephen Blackpool, a central figure in his story, were cruelly victim-ized by their fellows. . . .

[In his writing, Dickens satirized the employers.] He was not wholly opposed to their belief that an industrial society must be competitive and that the prosperity of the owners and the workers is intricately involved. It was the creed of the philosophic Radicals, typified by James Mill, that free trade between nations and free contract between individuals with no interference by legislators or trade unions was the right economic policy for both parties. Dickens was not of that persuasion. He was a Radical reformist not a *laissez-faire* [no government interference] theorist. But in writing an article for *Household Words* in February 1854 he called the Lancashire strike "a deplorable calamity" and "a great na-tional affliction", wasting energy and wages as well as wealth. He also lamented "the gulf of separation which it hourly deepens between those whose interests must be un-derstood to be identical or must be destroyed." In that sen-tence, whose full implication he may not have fully realized, he was asserting the essential interdependence of capital and labour. He was never a socialist. State ownership means more power for the Civil Service and governing Boards which were continually exposed to his scorn.

It may be asked what did he, as a social reformer, de-mand. The answer is decency and generosity. "Political economy", he wrote, "is a mere skeleton unless it has a little human covering and filling out, a little human bloom upon it and a little human warmth in it." By his insistence on the word "little" he was making a moderate as well as a rather vague request. It was not one likely to make any impact on the Gradgrinds. But general shame at the existing industrial conditions was growing, and Dickens did much to stir the public conscience. He was mellowing the climate of opinion. *Hard Times* has not been thought one of his better books. . . . But it was a further stimulant to the rejection of unfeeling individualism. Dickens could not solve the problem set by a capitalism which had the support of the "Manchester School" academics on a high level while it satisfied the cupidity [greed] of ruthless employers on a lower one. But he could and did create awareness that the problem existed and he reached the complacent middle class who were happily ignoring it. . . .

PRISONS AND PUNISHMENTS

A gaol [jail] loomed over Dickens when he was still a child.

"Shades of the prison-house begin to close
    Upon the growing Boy."

[Poet William] Wordsworth had seen with his imagination the material world and the advancing years as forms of incarceration. Dickens had his young experience of the grimly enclosing walls and the castle of despair when, as a boy of twelve, he was alternating his walk to work at the blacking-factory with visits to his father in the Marshalsea [prison]. John Dickens was out of the debtors' prison in three months and the son was released from his drudgery in less than five. But both were abiding and searing memories in his life. He was a prison-haunted man from the apprentice years in journalism to those of the established master. Penal reform was urgently needed and found vigorous support from one who had been so closely acquainted with the follies and cruelties of the gaols.

The visit of "Boz" [Dickens's pen name] to Newgate Gaol drove into the heart of darkness. When the mood of *Pickwick Papers* changed from the gaiety of the picaresque [fiction dealing with the adventures of a rogue] to the angry and sombre reporting of conditions in the Fleet Prison, he made his protest at the squalor of the broken lives. Twenty years later the horrors of confinement were to be the foreground and background of *Little Dorrit*, in which the gaol is a continuing symbol of a world in bondage to stupidity and greed. . . .

Imprisonment for debt is a major theme in *Pickwick Papers* and *Little Dorrit.* The system was absurd. When creditors took action the debtor was first removed to a sponging-house, an establishment kept by a bailiff or sheriff's officer. There he remained in some comfort for a short period in the hope that friends or relations would settle his affairs. If no money arrived he went to prison. Colonel Crawley in [William Makepeace] Thackeray's *Vanity Fair* was rescued by his wife from a sponging-house. He had not been suffering privation in Mr. Moss's "mansion in Cursitor Street." There was "a tably-de-hoty at half-past five with a little cards and music afterwards." John Dickens was removed by his son from a sponging-house, also in Cursitor Street, in 1834 and so escaped, through the generosity of Charles, from another spell in a debtors' prison.

If a gaoled debtor had money coming in, he could rent a room of his own and have food, drink and furniture brought in. For such a person the prison was a kind of compulsory lodging, shabby but tolerable. Mr Pickwick in the Fleet and John Dickens in the Marshalsea were thus accommodated. Those who had no money were massed together with nothing to do and very little to eat. They were scantily fed by charity. Outside the Fleet was a box, "a kind of iron cage", for receipt of donations. There was no opportunity for a prisoner to earn money and pay his debts. He might dwindle and decay for years while his creditors got nothing. Both parties were bound to lose. Reform of this nonsensical arrangement had to come. Debts over twenty pounds involved prison sentences until 1861 and gaoling for debt was not formally ended until 1869. The Dickensian revelations worked tardily, but they were effective in time.

CAPITAL PUNISHMENT

In his attitude to punishment, deterrence was accepted as the governing purpose, but his general belief in "benevolence" made him critical of the penal severity which degraded more than it deterred. Capital punishment he had long attacked but at the end of his life he accepted it in cases of murder as a necessary safeguard of society. During his boyhood there had been over two hundred capital offences, but there was a series of reductions of this terrible total during his early life as a writer. In 1837, after the "Boz" account of Newgate, the number fell to fifteen. In 1861 the crimes leading to the gallows were reduced to four, murder, treason, piracy, and arson in naval dockyards and arsenals.

Until 1868 executions for murder could be public spectacles. Dickens himself had seen two; a protesting critic had to know the facts of this national disgrace if he were to denounce it effectively. In 1849 he was one of a party who had paid two guineas a head for a place above the scaffold in Southwark when Mr [Frederick] and Mrs [Maria] Manning were the victims. He went, of course, in order to strengthen his campaign against the demoralizing results of such exhibitions. He saw the spectators and was appalled at their levity. His letters to *The Times,* describing the sadistic rejoicing of a debauched crowd including girls and boys, did not at once prevail despite the excitement which they caused. Once more the public conscience was slowly, but at last effectively, moved. Two years before his death he knew that such a disgusting raree-show could never happen again.

POVERTY AND THE POOR LAW

In 1837 Dickens was working on *Oliver Twist.* The Poor Law of 1834 had recently stringently altered the treatment of poverty and paupers. It had rationalized an anarchy of muddled and wasteful relief. The philosophic Radicals and political economists approved of the new measure because it seemed logical. Dickens, as a popular Radical, thought it brutal and ridiculed its National Commissioners, its boards of guardians and their officials; the last of these were typified in the obtuse and callous beadle, Bumble.

The novel did more than satirize a species and plant the word Bumbledom in the language. It indicted a whole system of workhouse incarceration which the Act was putting into force and which, despite his attack, remained in force. Twenty-eight years after *Oliver Twist* he drew the picture of the outcast but stubbornly proud Betty Higden who would rather die than go into "the House". In a postscript to *Our Mutual Friend* he said

> I believe there has been in England, since the days of the Stuarts, no law so often infamously administered, no law so often openly violated, no law habitually so ill-supervised. In the majority of the shameful cases of disease and death from destitution that shock the Public and disgrace the country, the illegality is quite equal to the inhumanity—and known language could say no more of their lawlessness.

Humphry House commented on this protest: "No genuine

attempt to meet his objections to the Poor Law was made until the appointment of the Royal Commission of 1905." That Dickens toiled in vain was not wholly true; the handling of pauper children was not so abominable at the end of his life. But there was no major reform.

The measure of 1834 had been devised to end the scandal of a system which originated during the hard times and rising prices of the Napoleonic wars. This allowed workers to draw a dole for themselves and families varying according to the price of bread. This was paid for out of the local rates. It was obviously a subsidy to employers who could thus keep down wages at other people's expense. The ending of that injustice without a sufficient rise in wages meant bitter hardship for the poor. The able-bodied had to work in penury [poverty]; if there was no food for their dependants they could go into the workhouses controlled by boards of guardians who were often chiefly guarding the tax-payers and determined to spend as little as possible on the inmates. In that they succeeded. The national burden of Poor Relief was rapidly reduced. The paupers paid for that by the miserable accommodation and strictly regulated diet which awaited them if they "went inside". G.M. [George Macaulay] Trevelyan in his *English Social History* decided that "Imperfect and harsh as was the Poor Law in 1834 it had been intellectually honest within its limits and contained the seeds of its own reform." To the popular hatred of the Law Dickens was a powerful stimulant. He could not accelerate the product of the seeds.

In *Oliver Twist* it was alleged by Dickens that pauperism at all ages was reduced by the simple process of starvation. More deaths meant less cost. His picture was a caricature. The No. 1 Dietary authorized by the Commissioners in 1836 included meat, fifteen ounces a week, soup and cheese along with the daily ration of a thin porridge called gruel. Twelve ounces of bread were issued daily. It was dismal fare, limited and starchy. Oliver's famous request for a second helping of gruel made fictional history. What is not explained is how the boy survived the starvation described. The story needed him and so he had to keep alive—against all probability.

With more success Dickens denounced the sale of pauper children as chimney-sweeps. It was only by accident that Oliver escaped being one of "the climbing boys" who were sent, often driven, up the flues by lighting a fire underneath them. "It's humane", said the scoundrel Gamfield, Oliver's prospective employer. "Even if they've stuck in the chimbley [chimney] roasting their feet makes them struggle to hextricate [extricate] themselves."

Parliament fumbled with the problem of ending these wicked apprenticeships. An Act passed in 1840 did not prevent evasion by employers. It failed and another Act was passed in 1864. Even so there had to be further legislation in 1875. No less horrible was the enslavement of apprentice children in the coalmines where, "chained and belted and harnessed like dogs, crawling as they dragged heavy loads behind them", they presented an appearance "indescribably disgusting and unnatural." That was not the verdict of a campaigning novelist. It was the report of a Commission of Inquiry. In 1842, thanks to Ashley Cooper, an Act restricted the underground employment of boys. The age-limit was put at ten!

MILLS AND FACTORIES

As a Londoner the young Dickens knew little of the new industrialism sprawling over and befouling those areas of the Midlands and the North which overlaid or adjoined the coalfields. The capital had its abundance of offices, shops, warehouses and craftsmen's premises where long hours of work were taken for granted. The London of "Boz" and the novels is a jostle of lively individuals rich in what the Elizabethans called "humours" [behavioral characteristics]. There was much self-employment by independent people. The town as Dickens saw it was not a swarming-ground of faceless "hands" and mass-produced and regimented proletarians. That kind of existence, teeming round pit-heads and factory chimneys, he soon met and found repulsive.

With *Oliver Twist* behind him and an unknown affluence attained, he was free to travel. He took the coach to the Midlands, sampled the tranquillity of Leamington and Warwick, and then encountered the Black Country where the machinery clattered and the furnaces burned night and day. It was "a mass of misery and dirt". To the boy from the cherry-ripe Kentish landscape and the still semi-rural London suburbs, here was a vision of hell, and his record of the horror is stamped in ink and gall on the central pages of *The Old Curiosity Shop*. He went on to Manchester where he saw what were said to be the best and worst of the cotton-mills and declared them to be both alike. He wrote in a letter to Edward Fitzgerald that he had been "disgusted beyond measure and meant to strike the heaviest blow possible for the unfortunate creatures in the factory towns". Yet, except in his reaction to the Midlands, where an outbreak of mob-violence was as odious to him as was the system which evoked it, he did not for a long time produce the promised novel about industrial conditions. He knew that his readers expected the tragi-comical vein and the blend of laughter with tears and of satire with sentiment. At Manchester he had met squalor of which he did not write and kind hearts, those of the Grant brothers, who became his Cheerybles [characters in *Nicholas Nickleby*], of whom he did write. The horrors of the industrial vortex had so distressed him that he wanted time before he struck.

When he returned to journalism as, briefly, the editor of the *Daily News* in 1846 and, with continuity, in charge of his own creation *Household Words* in 1850 he kept his earlier promise of "the heaviest possible blow." The inadequacy of the Factory Acts was frequently his theme. The delayed attack was fierce when it came.

The Reform Parliament, many of whose debates Dickens reported, passed a Factory Act in 1833. This expanded the feeble protection of young people provided by the Cotton Mills Act of 1819. It restricted the hours of employed children. But boys, many of them subjects of the virtual slavery of the apprenticeship already described, could still begin work at the age of nine. Their day in mills and factories was limited—and it is hard to believe now—to thirteen and a half hours of which one and a half were meal-breaks.

Regulation is useless without vigilance to enforce it and previously the inspection of factories was only the spare-time and amateur occupation of magistrates and clergymen. Evasion by unscrupulous employers was easy and frequent. The Act of 1833 arranged visiting by competent officials who had a legal right of entry to working premises. In 1842 came Cooper's Mines Act, previously mentioned, and in 1845 the same champion of the victims of industry won a valuable series of reforms. His Act of that year forbade night work for women and contained rules for the safety, meal-times and holidays of the young. That these orders were wantonly disobeyed is shown by Dickens's exposure of the disgraceful number of accidents in an article called "Ground in the Mill" written for *Household Words* in 1854. Young and old workers were "caught in the machinery and belting and smashed a hundred and twenty times a minute against the ceiling". Two thousand deaths and mutilations were reported in a period of six months and it is likely that many more were never reported at all.

When Dickens founded *Household Words* in 1850 he was part-owner and so had a power which he lacked during his short and stormy editorship of the *Daily News*. He was his own master and could develop his own ideas. His policy was to win a large public. The *Daily News* had begun with a circulation of only four thousand. *Household Words* had soon reached a sale of one hundred thousand.

It was designed to mingle pleading for causes with writing that pleased. The doctrinal element was prudently kept small. The editor, able to call on the liveliest journalists and best writers of fiction, was not going to let his vast public feel that they were being swamped with humanitarian propaganda. He called his creation "the gentle mouthpiece of reform" and demanded of his contributors "brightness, more brightness". His own articles were often far from gentle, but his editorial method gratified the middle-class magazine readers with its wide range of topics. Having been entertained they were more ready to be instructed on political and social issues. Attacking abuses can become a bore if the writers are obsessed with their own purposes and fall into monotonous preaching. . . . [Dickens] drove at the heart in order to plant the roots of radicalism in households for whom the fiction was cordial while the factual message was injected. Thus he continually assisted the campaigners who were slowly achieving reforms through legislation and administration. . . .

DICKENS'S OPTIMISM

"The pessimistic reformer dwells upon the fact that souls are being lost while the optimistic reformer dwells on the fact that they are worth saving. The first describes how bad men are under bad conditions, the second how good they are under bad conditions." Thus wrote [novelist and critic] G.K. Chesterton when considering the optimism of Dickens. It is a just tribute to a man who saw the progress of his desired reforms impeded and delayed by "the people governing" and yet retained his belief in "the people governed." He never white-washed a poor scoundrel simply because he was poor and politically powerless. He was not a determinist who believed that the only sins are those of society. He never pretended that poverty and innocence went together. When villainy was to be depicted in black colouring he laid on the sepia [brown coloring] whatever the rank of a cruel and corrupt rogue. But amid all the inhumanity of his time he never lost his faith in human nature. Some might think of his optimism as moon-struck and starry-eyed. But, as Chesterton pointed out in another essay, to look at a puddle on a dirty pavement is to see the moon reflected if the sky is clear and the lamps if it is not. To keep an eye on street-level does not mean dark despair. . . .

The raw material of social progress he provided with his anger and his imagination. Feelings, not figures, were his arsenal. It was the Fabian [anti-revolutionary socialist] [George Bernard] Shaw, once briefly a Marxist but soon "lapsed", who wrote of *Little Dorrit* that it was "a more seditious book than [Karl Marx's] *Das Kapital*. All over Europe men and women are in prison for pamphlets and speeches which are to *Little Dorrit* as red-pepper to dynamite." Shaw also said, wrongly of the novelist but rightly of the publicist, "If Dickens's day as a sentimental romancer is over, his day as a social prophet and social critic is only dawning." He added that the England of Thackeray and [Anthony] Trollope had gone but Dickens's England is "the real England we live in."

Horrified by violence and instinctively hostile to authoritarian rule, Dickens would have detested the results of the Marxist dynamite which exploded in eastern Europe and Asia. But in his gusts of laughter and in his majestic indignation he was the Victorian dynamo of reform. "The Inimitable", he liked to be called. He was also the Unquenchable.

The Social Impact of Dickens's Novels

Louis Cazamian

Dickens was highly critical of many aspects of Victorian society, as is evident in his writings. Whether or not these writings were actually effective in bringing about the reforms he so passionately advocated is more difficult to ascertain. The research needed to assess Dickens's impact on reform legislation was undertaken by Louis Cazamian, the distinguished French literary scholar, who wrote, among other works, an acclaimed study of the nineteenth-century English social novel, from which this excerpt is taken.

Cazamian's methodology was to compare British law before and after the publication of Dickens's works. Cazamian was thus able to demonstrate that, with regard to those issues under investigation, there was a marked improvement that could be attributed to Dickens. Obviously, Dickens could not single-handedly influence the enactment of laws for the amelioration of society; few people are capable of having such a dramatic impact on others. However, Dickens lived at a time when demands for social, political, and economic reforms were already widespread. Dickens's fiction, together with articles he published in the journals which he edited, invigorated these demands, bringing them to the attention of a wider and more influential public, including those who were not only able to introduce more liberal legislation in Parliament but were also able to ensure that reform bills were passed.

The philosophy of Christmas is a powerful, if confused, encouragement of social altruism [unselfishness, regard for others]. It exhibits the best qualities of Dickens's heart, and

Louis Cazamian, *The Social Novel in England 1830–1850: Dickens, Disraeli, Mrs. Gaskell, Kingsley,* translated by Martin Fido. Boston, MA: Routledge & Kegan Paul, 1973. Copyright © 1973 by Routledge & Kegan Paul. Reproduced by permission.

all the limitations of his head. But although he had no real knowledge of economics and, in his biographer's words, "He had not made politics at any time a study, and they were always an instinct with him rather than a science," he had the compensating gift of artistic vision, and an imaginative sensitivity which saw the whole human condition in any individual example of distress. He could comprehend some social evils and portray them so vividly that no one could fail to recognise them thereafter. Indeed, Dickens's vigorous criticism of certain abuses played a large part in the philanthropic improvement of social life in England.

EDUCATION AND NURSING

The more precisely defined were the attacks he launched on specific targets, of course, the more obvious were his tangible results. *Nicholas Nickleby* put an end to the worst abuses of the State's lack of concern with education. The Yorkshire schools had a detestable reputation; Dickens had heard tell of them in his childhood, and had never forgotten it: "I was always curious about Yorkshire schools—fell, long afterwards and at sundry times, into the way of hearing more about them—at last, having an audience, resolved to write about them." Thus, in this instance, the didactic [intended to teach or instruct] element was the starting-point of the novel. Dickens took a trip to Yorkshire to collect material, and searched the newspapers for reports of civil actions brought against the Yorkshire schoolmasters. He devoted the first few chapters of the book to the theme, and the public was magically affected by his forceful, moving account of the life of "the young gentlemen" at Dotheboys Hall, Squeers's ruffianly brutality, and the assistant master's misfortunes. Dickens's inimitable humor cast additional charm over all this, and the whole nation's attention was caught, with the result that the worst schools had to close down. It was at this point that the State began to take a hand in public education, and increased the miserly grants it had previously made. Circumstances favoured the movement, which was not to be halted. "There were then, a good many cheap Yorkshire schools in existence. There are very few now," wrote Dickens in 1867.

Similarly, Mrs Sarah Gamp and Mrs Betsy Prig, the unforgettable sick-nurses in *Martin Chuzzlewit*, were national figures as soon as they were created. They were coarse, bibulous [addicted to drinking], unconscientious, and utterly cynical in their exploitation of sickness and death: public opinion accepted this as just criticism of nursing, whose failings had been disregarded for too long. Thenceforth, private initiative and public administration were united in their efforts to correct the abuses of nursing, and by 1900 the nursing force was one of the country's outstanding welfare institutions.

Mention must be made here of Dickens's influence on education in the widest sense. The emotional current of his writings, with their stress on family affection, their charming treatment of children as characters, and the realisation of the unhappiness of ill-treated children, helped to introduce a gentler spirit into educational practices. This is brought out, and perhaps exaggerated, in J.L. Hughes's book, *Dickens as an Educator*:

> It will be admitted that he has done more than any one else to secure for the child a considerate treatment of his tender age. "It is a crime against a child to rob it of its childhood." This principle was announced by Dickens, and it has come to be generally recognised and adopted.

PRISONS

Dickens's agitation was most successful in the legal sphere. Prisons and the penal system were a perpetual preoccupation of his, experience having given him an intimate knowledge of the subject. As we have seen, ideas for reform were in the air. Dickens's merit was not that of a pioneer or original thinker; he lent his incomparable literary support to reforms which had already been started, and there can be no doubt that he expedited their completion. He often denounced the cruelty of the penal code, as he does, for example, in Dennis the hangman's story in *Barnaby Rudge*:

> Mary Jones, a young woman of nineteen who come up to Tyburn with a infant at her breast, and was worked off for taking a piece of cloth off the counter of a shop in Ludgate-Hill, and putting it down again when the shopman see her, and who had never done any harm before, and only tried to do that, in consequence of her husband having been pressed [impressed, forced to serve in British army or navy] three weeks previous, and she being left to beg, with two young children—as was proved upon the trial.

Still more, he attacked the unequal treatment of rich and poor at the hands of the law. . . . *Hard Times* faces the problem of divorce squarely, and asks whether it is right that this should be the prerogative of the rich. *Oliver Twist* is a protracted complaint about the law's pointless severity with the downtrodden. Dickens played a large part in the suppression of public executions. In one episode in *Dombey and Son* he evokes pity for the lot of the infanticide mother, who has been lightly seduced and abandoned. Themes like these recur insistently while, as we know, the law's severities underwent parallel curtailment.

No one did more to reform debtors' prisons. Unlike bankrupts, insolvents [people unable to pay their debts] had their persons seized and their future income attached [seized] by their creditors. The state of their prisons was unbelievable: the law made no provision for minimal material, hygienic, or moral conditions to be maintained for the unfortunate prisoners. The public was indignant about the situation: the Court established by the Act of 1813 had released 50,000 debtors over thirteen years, one of its beneficiaries being Dickens's father at the end of his spell in the Marshalsea, where Dickens saw the conditions on occasional visits. But there were still very many prisoners under lock and key: in 1827, 6,000 people were arrested for debt in London alone. The law commissioners declared in 1830 that the widespread objections to the insolvency laws were justified. It was at this point that Dickens stepped in, and painted a convincing picture of the corrupting boredom of a pointless existence, the demoralising spectacle of rich debtors buying privileges, and all the cruelty of a system of debilitating, impoverished inactivity. Mr Pickwick's incarceration in the Fleet Prison served as a pretext for a lively tragi-comic description of this particular world:

> We still leave unblotted in the leaves of our statute-book, for the reverence and admiration of succeeding ages, the just and wholesome law which declares that the sturdy felon shall be fed and clothed, and that the penniless debtor shall be left to die of starvation and nakedness.

Later, in *Little Dorrit*, Dickens returned to the theme and exhibited the moral anguish of Marshalsea prisoners to thousands of readers. But by that time he was describing the past; reform had come swiftly after the publication of *Pickwick* in 1837. A measure to soften the law's rigour was put forward in 1838, but was thrown out. In 1844, after repeated efforts, Cottenham succeeded in bringing the penalties for debt closer to those for bankruptcy.

LAWYERS AND THE LAW

Dickens satirised the failings of lawyers and the law without mercy, and by now his criticisms are seen to have been correct. After the publication of *Pickwick*, the devious figures of Dodson and Fogg and the immortal case of *Bardell v. Pickwick* suggested that the author had a distinctly limited respect for legal cunning and its practitioners. In *Oliver Twist* we are shown Mr Fang, the police court magistrate, whose brutal method of dispensing summary justice is made an eloquent protest, as Dickens portrays it. *The Old Curiosity Shop* introduces the characteristic figures of the attorney, Sampson Brass, and his sister Sally: a delightful pair who turn his slipperiness and her tartness against the letter and spirit of the law. *David Copperfield* takes us into Doctors' Commons and the old legal firms which cynically exploit their clients. *Bleak House,* in the last analysis, is a formidable attack upon the spirit, conduct, and very existence of the Court of Chancery. Here again the writer's strictures [critical remarks] were amply justified: public attention had been focused on the weaknesses of Chancery for a long time. Its endless delays, enormous costs, incessantly renewable appeals and countersuits, and exhaustingly complicated procedures were proverbial. We know from the author's Preface and Forster's research that the case of Gridley, "the man from Shropshire", was based on an actual suit. "What a mockery of justice this is," wrote the author of the pamphlet on which Dickens drew:

> The facts speak for themselves, and I can personally vouch for their accuracy. The costs already incurred in reference to this £300 legacy are not less than from £800 to £900, and the parties are no forwarder. Already near five years have passed by, and the plaintiff would be glad to give up his chance of the legacy if he could escape from his liability to costs, while the defendants who own the little farm left by the testator, have scarce any other prospect before them than ruin.

Two public letters addressed to Dickens in 1859 show the extent to which public opinion was behind him: the anonymous author asserted that he, like many others, was not only warmly attached to Dickens for the deep impression his books had made on him, but also for the implacable hatred he had always shown for the Court of Chancery as it existed then—a monster of iniquity [wickedness]. The book [*Bleak House*] may not have had an immediate effect, but for a long time legal practitioners were sensitive to its criticism of their ways, and it played its part in the reorganisation of the High Courts in 1873.

INTERVENTIONISM

Elsewhere, when he was attacking less clear-cut targets, and describing complex evils, it is harder to demonstrate any direct Dickensian influence. His personal achievement here was merged with that of contemporaries working in the same sphere. But certainly it was an element in the moral evolution of interventionism [any interference that affects the affairs or interests of others], although we are reduced to conjecture when we try to deduce its precise importance. The popularity of Dickens's books, and his undoubted hold over his readers' hearts and minds, are evidence that such importance existed.

Two Contradictory Views of Society in Dickens's Work

Kate Flint

Writers, even great writers, sometimes make assumptions about society (and human nature) that,
when subjected to close scrutiny and investigation,
seem to be logically incompatible, even conflicting.
A critical reading of Dickens's novels reveals such
conflicting assumptions. On the one hand, Dickens
regarded people as products of their environment,
trapped by their past, and thus unable to change. Yet
on the other hand, he expressed a more positive
view, namely that given the will to do so, individuals
had the ability to change themselves and to trans-
form society. The two opposing views of human nature—determinism and free will—represent different
philosophical concepts that have been debated
through the ages and, despite persuasive arguments
for each, have never easily been reconciled.

These assumptions about society and human nature underlie the following analysis of Dickens's am-
bivalence, written by Kate Flint, tutor in English at
Oxford University, and taken from her critical study
of Dickens's novels.

Dickens' novels clearly express ambivalent attitudes towards those who, in the past, had wished to change things.
Standing still or, worse still, retrogression are presented as
highly undesirable. But the dramatisation of those who go
about trying to change things the *wrong* way is both more
alluring in the literary opportunities which it offers, and requires less effort of analytical imagination than putting forward favourable modes of change. This is particularly ap-

parent when Dickens moves to the problems of his own time. Here, moreover, he seems to be caught between two competing social theories, both of which are present but neither of which is dominant within his work. The one asserts that people are products of their environment, of their education. It is a belief closely linked to an acknowledgement of the entrapping power of the past. Yet the other theory which Dickens' fiction tries to demonstrate is that change is not only possible, but that it can take place within an individual, and that wider social change may well have its most profitable source in the stimulation of individual sympathy and will to action. This can only be possible if human qualities are something innate, can be acted upon, and are independent of environmental determination.

DICKENS' AMBIVALENCE

As Raymond Williams has pointed out in his essay "The Reader in *Hard Times*," these two incompatible ideological positions can be related to different intellectual and social strands. The former views were those argued by the rationalist philosophers [William] Godwin and [Robert] Owen; the latter were those held by many Christians. Williams goes on to note that both positions are powerfully present in *Hard Times*. "The Godwinian version of a shaping environment, in family and very specifically in education, is there from the beginning in the Gradgrind philosophy and M'Choakumchild's school." The fact that environment can determine a whole community is suggested by the fact that we move from the streets being "all very like one another" to the people being "equally like another." On the other hand, Stephen Blackpool and Rachael seem, somehow, to have survived unscathed from their systemic surroundings. Moreover, it is not sufficient to shrug one's shoulders when reading and suggest that this apparent incompatibility can be summed up by Blackpool's phrase, that it's "aw a muddle." For the novel doesn't just present confused, conflicting ideals, suggesting that "life" is like this. It attempts answers, and

> great stress is laid on both ways out of the situation: the loving way of Sissy Jupe, the way reached by Louisa and even, in part, by Gradgrind, the way of suffering of Rachael—"heart" and the "change of heart"; but also the way of a reformed educational system, teaching "fancy" as well as "fact", and of a reformed economic and social system, moving beyond self-interest to mutual duty and community.

At its most clearcut in *Hard Times*, this duality is found throughout Dickens' novels. It meshes with further contradictions—for example Dickens' belief, at times, that there is a social system (or systems) in need of reformation; and the dislike of systems. . . . It is a form of ideological uncertainty which leaves the reader perplexed. For the tone of the texts, the modes of address, seem to be prodding the Victorian addressees not just to response, but into action. Yet what responses, and what actions, do the novels ask of them?

THE LONDON POOR

Dickens was credited by his contemporaries with being the writer who, before all others, enabled and stimulated a kind of sympathetic literary voyeurism towards the lives of the poor and the London poor in particular. It was due to him, commented Harriet Beecher Stowe, visiting England in 1853, that "Fashionable literature now arrays itself on the side of the working classes." Later, in 1862, Margaret Oliphant surveyed recent English literature in the pages of *Blackwood's Edinburgh Magazine:*

> Mr. Dickens was one of the first popular writers who brought pictures of what is called common life into fashion. It is he who has been mainly instrumental in leading the present generation of authors to disregard to a great extent the pictorial advantages of life on the upper levels of society, and to find a counterpicturesqueness in the experiences of the poor . . . He has made washerwomen as interesting as duchesses.

ALLEVIATING POVERTY

Dickens took an active part in certain causes concerned with the amelioration of social conditions, and was publicly seen, and known to be active in such campaigns. Notably, . . . he was associated with Angela Burdett-Coutts's Urania Cottage, the home she established with the intention of reforming prostitutes, and with her plans for a model housing project in Nova Scotia Gardens, one of the most notorious areas of Bethnal Green. He used his journalism to publicise specific abuses, such as the conditions which led to the deaths of 159 children from cholera in the Tooting workhouse. His brother-in-law, Henry Austin, was general secretary of the Board of Health. Dickens was in regular correspondence with him and the pioneering health and sanitation reformer, Edwin Chadwick. In 1846, Dickens wrote to Lord Morpeth in the hope of obtaining some public employment or com-missionership in this field—a fact which provides a check to easy generalisations about his distrust of public bodies:

> On any questions connected with the Education of the People, the elevation of their character, the improvement of their dwellings, their greater protection against disease and vice— or with the treatment of Criminals, or the administration of Prison Discipline, which I have long observed closely—I think I could do good service, and I am sure I should enter with my whole heart.

Nothing came of this request, but Dickens' desire to have a magazine of his own was to a large degree prompted by his wish to see a forum where these issues could be put before a wide public.

In his earlier writings, . . . Dickens highlighted particular issues: the Sabbath bills in *Sunday Under Three Heads;* the poverty and despair which drive people to alcoholism in "Gin Shops" in *Sketches by Boz;* debtors' prisons in *Pickwick Papers;* and the notorious Yorkshire schools in *Nicholas Nickleby.* That is not to say that, in this earlier fiction, he did not occasionally glance sideways at the wider implications of the existence of specific malpractices. In *Nicholas Nickleby,* to take perhaps the most outstanding example, Nicholas, pacing the streets, despondent with personal troubles, tries to put these problems into their true perspective, reflecting, among other things,

> how in seeking, not a luxurious and splendid life, but the bare means of a most wretched and inadequate subsistence, there were women and children in that one town, divided into classes, numbered and estimated as regularly as the no-ble families and folks of great degree, and reared from in-fancy to drive most criminal and dreadful trades—how igno-rance was punished and never taught—how jail door gaped, and gallows loomed for thousands urged towards them by circumstances darkly curtaining their very cradles' heads, and but for which they might have earned their honest bread and lived in peace—how many died in soul, and had no chance of life . . . when he thought of all this, and selected from the mass the one slight case on which his thoughts were bent, he felt indeed that there was little ground for hope, and little cause or reason why it should not form an atom in the huge aggregate of distress and sorrow, and add one small and unimportant unit to swell the great amount.

But it is precisely in opposition to seeing human conditions and social problems in terms of units and amounts that Dick-ens puts forward, throughout his novels, the possibility and desirability of individual effort, benevolence and charity.

According to Forster, it was in the 1840s that the notion of individual regeneration came to lodge firmly in Dickens' fiction. This was a time when "the hopelessness of any true solution of either political or social problems by the ordinary Downing-street methods" was startlingly impressed upon him by Carlyle's writings, as well as by his own observations, with the result that he began to try to "convert society" by showing that its happiness rested on "the same foundations as those of the individual, which are mercy and charity no less than justice". Dickens' attitude did not change significantly in subsequent years. Moreover, as his speeches, and as such studies as Philip Collins' *Dickens and Crime* have amply shown, his belief in the need to maintain the class system as it was became, at least in his overt pronouncements, increasingly entrenched. What angered him most . . . was a lack of acceptance of mutual responsibility among its constituent parts. Any such acceptance cannot be legislated for; it must, for Dickens, take place at an individual level and, like all the best reform, radiate outwards. However powerful his writing might have been at pointing to abuses, he offers no radical surgery.

ON INDUSTRIALISM

One reason for this is a simple one. Indivisible from Dickens' support for the existing class structure—a structure which did, as he saw it, allow for individual activity and economic enterprise—was the fact that although Dickens might attack the working and living conditions to which industrialism could give rise, he did not come out against the growth and development of manufacturing industry *per se.* He was no Luddite [one who advocates destroying machinery], no [John] Ruskin, prophesying in 1859 a nightmare vision of the twentieth century, with

> the whole of the island . . . set as thick with chimneys as the masts stand in the docks of Liverpool; that there shall be no meadows in it; no trees; no gardens; only a little corn grown upon the house tops, reaped and thrashed by steam; that you do not even have room for roads, but travel either over the roofs of your mills, on viaducts; or under their floors, in tunnels; that, the smoke having rendered the light of the sun unserviceable, you work always by the light of your own gas: that no acre of English ground shall be without its shaft and its engine.

. . . Indeed, in a speech of 1865, Dickens listed Luddite actions in a long summary of the social evils which had afflicted the country in relatively recent times, but which now, happily, had disappeared: he spoke against "the destruction of machinery which was destined to supply unborn millions with employment". In fact, he heartily approved of much to do with the operation and consequences of industrialisation.

CHAPTER 3

DICKENS'S DEVELOPMENT AS A WRITER

PEOPLE WHO MADE HISTORY

CHARLES DICKENS

From Escapism to Social Realism

Ivor Brown

Jane Austen and Sir Walter Scott were both, in their own distinctive ways, representative of early–nineteenth-century British novelists: both refrained from making critical judgments of their society; both ignored the momentous political and economic events of their time. Jane Austen's subject matter was the social world of the upper middle classes, although for much of her life, the Napoleonic Wars were raging across Europe. Sir Walter Scott preferred to write romantic adventure novels set in past centuries, even though Britain was then rapidly industrializing.

Ivor Brown, author of a highly praised socio-historical biography of Dickens, maintains that Dickens changed the course of development of the English novel. In the following excerpt from *Dickens in His Time*, Brown discusses Dickens's writing within the context of Victorian society. Brown demonstrates that Dickens became concerned with the suffering of the poor and with the cruelty and injustice which they had to endure. Dickens chose to write about all classes of society, particularly the lower classes, instead of confining himself to the social comedy of a refined élite, as Jane Austen did. He wrote about contemporary England undergoing the ravages of the Industrial Revolution, instead of escaping to the age of chivalry and romance as Sir Walter Scott did.

For three thousand years the story-teller had excited and amused, or at the highest level of his work examined human character in all its fortitude and frailty. But it was the character of the individual that was probed and portrayed by this kind of authorship in various grades of quality. Shakespeare,

Ivor Brown, *Dickens in His Time*. London: Thomas Nelson and Sons, 1963.

to take the summit of achievement in this kind, was masterly in his study of the single man or woman; he did not set out to be what we call a student of society or a clamorous reformer. During his lifetime of fifty-two years there was a dynastic change: Queen Elizabeth died and James VI of Scotland and I of England united the two crowns. Commerce expanded and the population of the country grew slightly larger, and most of it grew no richer since the possessors remained in possession and the value of money declined. The anger of Shakespeare, who could be very angry, was directed at the vices of the individual, greed, pride, lechery, cruelty, and so on. His age knew all about the Deadly Sins and did not arraign the Deadly Society as so many writers were to do, with Dickens at the head of them, in the nineteenth and twentieth centuries.

JANE AUSTEN

The story-teller, or novelist as we say now, did not conceive it to be his or her business to use words as dynamite for blowing up the social order. Jane Austen, who died [in 1817] when Dickens was a boy of five, took the English country gentleman's way of life for granted. Napoleon might storm across Europe; but paying calls and party-giving would go serenely on. During the eventful years between 1796, when she began to write *Pride and Prejudice*, and her death in 1817 she held her sensitive mirror up to the foibles [weaknesses] of human nature as if there were no national or social problems. "Problem" is now a word of which we read and hear daily and almost hourly. The air, as well as newsprint, is full of eager and anxious people explaining and discussing their problems. But problems were no concern of the novelist until Dickens, beginning with journalism, started to mix his fictions with the facts of public misery and injustice and to make his stories a reformer's challenge as well as a feast of entertainment.

SIR WALTER SCOTT

A notable example of the novelist withdrawn from political and economic observation and from critical survey of the great contemporary changes in the state of the nation was Sir Walter Scott. During his sixty-one years of life (1771–1832) the face of central Scotland was being rapidly enriched and befouled with the onrush of the new steam-powered industries, fed with the local coal. Glasgow, long a useful harbour and a western outlet for the sailing-ships, was Britain's pioneer in steam navigation and speedily became a thriving centre of the new industrialism. Population grew rapidly and workers swarmed to the mills and factories. New families arose with a new economic power far exceeding the sway of the old clan chieftains. What a world for an observant man to write about! But Sir Walter, working in his Tweedside home, which he furnished and decorated as a medieval museum, turned his back on this urgent and superb subject, using the English as well as the Scottish history of many centuries past to provide the backgrounds for his huge outpouring of romances. Only in *St Ronan's Well* did he bring his fictions up to date, and then he did not go to the Clyde: he stayed in a Border spa. The steamers on the Clyde, the new surge of mingled wealth and poverty, and the creation of a brash and ugly Scotland were not for him. He could respond to a riot in Edinburgh if it were a hundred years old and could be viewed as history. The "pressing modern problem", if he saw it at all, was no concern of his.

But at the end of the eighteenth century the whole pace and strain of the common life were being intensified. The Industrial Revolution was properly so called. When steam-power set the wheels revolving it meant more wealth for some and less well-being for most. The crafts which had remained unchanged through the ages had a quality which machine production could not emulate. But quality ceased to count. The Age of Quantity had arrived, quantity of goods that were not so good, of money that multiplied itself by shrewd investment, and of crowds who flocked into the factory towns and bred plentifully amid the squalor. These towns were being built without plan or provision or scruples of any kind. The Age of Quantity was also the Age of Anyhow. . . .

DICKENS'S WRITING

Lord [George Gordon] Byron [a poet] did carry a protesting temper into the House of Lords and might have been a poet-politician had he stayed on in England. But his fashionable public wanted his biting wit and not his radical opinions and preferred the satirist to the rebel. He died for freedom in Greece [in 1824] when Dickens was a boy of twelve [who] had already seen the London of the workaday thousands in all its poverty, drudgery, and hunger as he worked in the

dark and rat-ridden premises of Warren's Blacking Warehouse at Hungerford Stairs near Charing Cross. Dickens was
not there very long, but the squalor and the misery remained
with him in bitter memories all his life and did much to determine the form which his writing was to take. This was fiction based on facts, the facts of a suddenly changing England,
where supremacy of the old families and their hangers-on
was being shared with the new lords of money and machinery, while the poor remained the poor. . . .

THE THEATER

What Dickens did for the novel by making it a critical survey
of his time as well as a gripping narrative was not done for
the theatre until some time after his death. [Henrik] Ibsen in
Norway [1828–1906] had begun with the old romantic saga-
subjects before he turned to realism and drove right into the
heart of the contemporary community, whose shams he was
determined to show up. Bernard Shaw [1856–1950] a boy
just on fourteen when Dickens died in 1870, later expounded
and championed Ibsen's attacks on the pillars and pretensions of society and carried on the work of exposure, using
the stage as his platform for attacking the old and false ideas
and ideals and proposing his remedies for the moral, economic, and political failures of the time. Shaw read Dickens
closely and knew the novels in detail. The two men differed
greatly in their temperaments and talents, but they had a
similar approach to their work. Nowadays they would be
called "social realists." When Shaw was told that the drama
should not try to teach people the business of living sensibly
and decently he curtly replied that it should do nothing else.
Dickens, since he was born a brilliant story-teller, would not
have gone so far as that, but he certainly regarded himself as
a man with a message and a mission and not simply as a
spinner of yarns. . . .

A NEW KIND OF NOVEL

The novelist who was to scourge [condemn] so many of the
abuses and the malefactors [evil-doers] of his age had suddenly emerged and immediately afterwards was to turn his
lash on to the greedy and brutish owners of boys' schools,
where unwanted children were deposited to rot in semi-
starvation and often to die of cold, hunger, and neglect. As
his work developed the whole tone and temper of the writ-

ing altered. The random pleasures provided by the picaresque [episodic] novel were left behind and the serious purpose of purging and punishing the scandals of the national life determined the nature of these books and of the work to come. Great gusts of laughter, sometimes almost a hurricane of hilarity, were still to roar through the length and strength of the vast Dickens stories. But the laughter was the companion of the verbal lash. And the characters, instead of being fantastic, become more actual.

Sir Walter Scott died in 1832 at a time when Dickens was establishing himself as a speedy and accurate reporter in the gallery of the House of Commons. In 1833 Dickens saw the first of his essay-sketches in print and began to follow this up under the pen-name of Boz with graphic studies of London life, some of them grim portraits of its ugliest side. In 1836 a selection of these was successfully published in book form. The mainly jovial *Pickwick Papers* began to appear in serial form in the same year. *Oliver Twist* followed in 1838 and *Nicholas Nickleby* in 1839. A new kind of novel had been born, a novel no longer rooted in the romantic past, like Scott's, or withdrawn from nine-tenths of current happenings, like Jane Austen's, but relevant to the hard facts of hard times in all their light and darkness and offering its readers not just a solace for idle hours but a challenge to their sense of right and wrong.

An Increasing Readership

Michael Wheeler

Michael Wheeler, head of the Department of English
at the University of Lancaster and co-editor of the
Longman Literature in English Series, has written a
study of Victorian literature from which the following excerpt is taken. Here Wheeler focuses attention
on the economic background to the production of
Victorian novels.

Novels published during the period under discussion, 1830–1890, rank among the greatest ever written in English. Yet there were several obstacles that
had to be overcome before a novel was published.
Each manuscript, handwritten, had to be approved
by the publisher and his reader, by the magazine editor (if published serially), by the lending library
proprietor, and by the bookseller, with the ultimate
success of a novel depending on the reading public.
Novels written in the first decades of the nineteenth
century tended to be long, generally three or four
volumes, and were thus costly to publish. In the
1830s, serial magazine publication, a system by
which a novel was published in numerous installments, reduced considerably the price of novels. Toward mid-century, the establishment of lending libraries suddenly made novels available to readers at
minimal expense, thereby increasing the availability
of books to the public.

The Victorian Age was not only the longest but also the
greatest in the history of English fiction. It was an age of the
novel in the same sense that the Restoration was an age of
drama and the Romantic period an age of poetry. The past
tense seems inappropriate, however, when one considers

Michael Wheeler, *English Fiction of the Victorian Period 1830–1890.* New York: Longman, 1985. Copyright © 1985 by Longman Group Limited. Reproduced by permission.

Novel-reading was a popular middle-class leisure activity in the nineteenth century. Novels, such as this one by Charles Dickens, were often read aloud in a family circle.

how much Victorian fiction is still in print, and is still read by the general reading public. . . .

THOUSANDS OF NOVELS

The "greatness" of this age of fiction is not only qualitative, however—a matter of a galaxy of major talent—but also quantitative. For the work of a host of other writers, ranging from Wilkie Collins to Rider Haggard, from [Benjamin] Disraeli to George Moore, and from Charles Kingsley to Mrs. Humphry Ward, still lives in the sense that it is still read, and is also the subject of closer critical attention today than at any time since its publication. Quantity in this context has another, negative side to it, of course, and most of the tens of thousands of novels published during Victoria's reign (an estimate of forty thousand is sometimes quoted) are unquestionably buried, if not dead and quite beyond recall. They lie in the catacombs of the major libraries, to be disturbed perhaps once or twice a century by scholars who seek more representative views of the age than the most original creative writers generally offer, or more representative examples of specific sub-genres. These forgotten novels have gone the way of all minor examples of popular literature written to pass the reader's time and keep the writer's pot boiling, or to instruct the reader and get the writer's pet theory into print. In an age which delighted in the clutter of Gothic architecture and heavily ornamental interior design, novels were all too often not so much "baggy monsters" as monstrous bags, into which almost anything could be crammed. Given that some kind of love interest was virtually a *sine qua non* [necessity], whether as the main theme, or as a side issue introduced for light relief, or, more interestingly, as a means whereby other themes—political, social, religious—could be domesticated, hundreds of minor writers published rambling novels in which every conceivable topic of the day was treated. Significantly, some of the writers of novels . . . would not have described themselves as novelists, but turned naturally to the most popular literary vehicle available.

ECONOMICS OF PUBLISHING

Under what conditions, then, were novels—major works of literature and pot-boilers alike—published in the nineteenth century? The fact that the Victorian novelist wrote for

THE NOVEL AND THE VICTORIAN MIDDLE CLASS

Alice Jenkins, lecturer in English at the University of Glasgow, and Juliet John, lecturer in English at the University of Salford, have co-edited a book on Victorian culture and also Rereading Victorian Fiction, *from which this excerpt is taken.*

Discussing the Victorian novel within a socioeconomic context, Jenkins and John point out that the readership of these novels was drawn from both the middle classes, who were already literate, as well as from the lower classes, who were increasingly becoming literate. As members of both classes became more politically involved, demanding parliamentary reform, their concerns were reflected in the novels of the period.

In 1837 the country [England] was in the midst of a cultural revolution, quieter perhaps than the political and industrial revolutions afoot, but no less formative in the emergence of the novel as the genre of the age—and formative, further, in the development of a modern state. Literacy was increasing and developments in the publishing trade meant that books and newspapers were expanding this readership, moving further down the social ladder in the early Victorian period than ever before. . . .

In 1831, Colburn and Bentley's Standard Novels were being published at six shillings each. These developments began a sharp fall in book prices leading to a broader readership, a trend which continued until 1850. The popularity and availability of the new literary form of the novel at the outset of the Victorian period in fact represents the beginnings of a mass readership.

The association of the novel with the middle class is not, then, a simple, monologic story of cultural imperialism. While the "rise" of the middle class is one of upward social mobility, the "rise" of the novel is very much bound up with economic and educational developments which allowed literature to move *down* the social ladder. Again, though the novel and the middle class may have dominated the social and cultural scene in the Victorian period, this very domination was itself in some respects a radical feature of Victorian history (though it should be remembered that in many ways the newly empowered middle class brought conservative and bourgeois values into political prominence). The middle class was an agent of change; its favourite genre, the novel, was reflective of that change.

Alice Jenkins and Juliet John, eds., *Rereading Victorian Fiction.* New York: St. Martin's Press, 2000, pp. 3–4.

the reading public rather than for a patron meant in effect that he or she had several masters rather than one: these might include the publisher and his professional "reader", the editor of a magazine, the proprietor of a circulating library, the bookseller, and, directly or indirectly, the reading public itself. . . . By the second decade of the nineteenth century, when Scott and Jane Austen were writing, novels were generally published in three or four volumes. Although three-volume novels, or "three-deckers", sold at a standard price of half a guinea a volume, which put them beyond the means of most middle-class readers, they remained the staple form throughout our period. The remarkable staying power of the three-decker has been attributed to the fact that it was commercially safe. Its success, however, and eventual demise also coincided with the rise and fall of Charles Edward Mudie, the mogul of the Victorian circulating libraries.

LENDING LIBRARIES

Mudie started lending books in a shop in Bloomsbury in 1842, and rapidly expanded his empire into the country and abroad. Books were lent a volume at a time for a fee of a guinea a year per reader. Voracious readers who could not afford expensive three-deckers could borrow them for a fraction of the retail price, bound in Mudie's own boards. Many aspiring writers also benefited, in that Mudie's order of a couple of hundred copies often represented the difference between the launching of a literary career and oblivion. Furthermore, if a novel were particularly successful with the reading public, Mudie would buy in more from the publisher and reserve a large stock of the author's next work. Usurping some of the publisher's power, Mudie also acted as an unofficial defender of public morals. . . . Mudie's own scrutiny of novels—a first level of screening— was supplemented by letters received from irate fathers and anxious clergymen complaining about books borrowed from his libraries, mainly by women, who made up the majority of the novel-reading public. The consequent withdrawal of titles sometimes had disastrous results for their authors.

Before the advent of radio and television, novel-reading, and particularly reading aloud in the family circle, were of course common middle-class leisure activities. . . .

Although cheap reprints of three-deckers often came out some years after the first edition, and "collective editions" of established novelists such as Dickens and [Edward] Bulwer [Lytton] were to be among the reasonably priced "railway" novels sold by W.H. Smith [a popular bookstore] from mid-century, new fiction was not read by anything like its potential readership in the 1830s until the revival of the monthly part novel, initiated by the publication of Dickens's *Pickwick Papers* (1836–37). An improvised miscellany which later turned into a novel, and which sold in huge numbers after the introduction of Sam Weller, *Pickwick* set the pattern for most of Dickens's later novels, as well as for those of some of his rivals. . . .

Clearly, then, we have to take cognizance of the form or forms in which Victorian novels were published. For although serial novels were reprinted in volumes, and, in the case of [Thomas] Hardy for example, were sometimes revised at that stage, the fact remains that most Victorian fiction was not originally written to be read throughout over a short space of time. Novelists' decisions on such matters as pace and the introduction of new characters were dictated partly by the demands of the specific form in which their work was to be serialized. The same is true for the writer of modern television drama. . . .

THE MARKET FOR BOOKS

Conditions were right for the production of large numbers of novels in the Victorian Age, not least because the Industrial Revolution had expanded and strengthened the position of the middle classes, who made up the majority of the novel-reading public. Urban growth had been rapid in the early decades of the century, and by 1841, 48.3 per cent of the population of England and Wales lived in towns and cities. By 1881 the figure had risen to 70.2 per cent. The combined effects of expansion in manufacture, commerce and overseas trade, increased movement of population, and improvements in transport systems, led to a broadening of the middle classes which now ranged from the lowly clerk to the captain of industry, and to considerable upward and downward social mobility, itself a favourite theme of the novelists. A vigorous working-class sub-culture, also the product of urbanization, supplied the needs of a social group which was less illiterate than is often imagined. It was not, however, until Forster's Education Act of 1870 had produced a more ambitious generation among the "lower orders" that novelists complained of the over-production of fiction to cater for this new readership. Broadly speaking, the English novel of the period everywhere reflects, while often also challenging, middle-class values.

The Serial Publication of Dickens's Novels

John Butt and Kathleen Tillotson

When Dickens's first novel, *Pickwick Papers,* appeared in print in 1836–1837, its method of publication marked a turning point in the availability of novels to the British public. *Pickwick Papers* was published in serial form: Episodes of thirty-two pages each appeared monthly for nineteen months, with the final installment being a double one. The method of serial publication had been used elsewhere, but it was not common in Britain until Dickens. After the success of his first novel, Dickens proceeded with the serial publication of a further eight novels. By enabling readers to purchase novels in episode form, serial publication reduced the expense of reading considerably, and as a consequence, readership of novels in Victorian England increased dramatically.

John Butt, professor of English at Edinburgh University, and Kathleen Tillotson, professor of English at London University, discuss serial publication in some detail in this excerpt from their classic critical study of Dickens's craft, *Dickens at Work.* They show that there were distinct disadvantages for the writer who published serially—among them, meeting monthly deadlines for publication and ensuring that each episode was enough of a "cliff-hanger" to retain reader interest. At the same time, serial publication tended to strengthen the bond between the author and his readers. Dickens not only received letters each month with readers' comments, but was able to gauge reader response to his work by the increase or decrease in monthly sales.

It is a commonplace in the criticism of early drama that the conditions in which a dramatist worked must be taken into

John Butt and Kathleen Tillotson, *Dickens at Work.* New York: Methuen, 1982. Copyright © 1957 by Methuen & Company, Ltd. Reproduced by permission.

account. He wrote for a theatre of a certain shape, with certain structural features, which permitted him to use certain dramatic effects. The analogy can be applied to the novelist who, though he has greater freedom than the dramatist, must also suit what he has to say to the current conventions of presentation. Just as Shakespeare thought in terms of a theatre without drop curtain, artificial lighting, or scenery, and of a theatrical company of male actors only, so Dickens was accustomed to think in terms of publication peculiar to his time. Today novels are customarily published in single volumes. A hundred and fifty years ago this form of publication was unusual. In the eighteenth century, novels had appeared in five volumes, or even in as many as seven; but by the time of Scott and Jane Austen the usual number was three or four. The prices varied: it was not uncommon to charge as much as half a guinea a volume, which made novel-reading exceedingly expensive to those who did not belong to a circulating library. These were still the conditions ruling when Dickens began to write. His first novel, *Pickwick Papers*, shows him attempting to reach a larger number of readers by cutting the price to suit their pockets. . . .

REDUCING THE EXPENSE OF READING

After the first few numbers of *Pickwick*, each monthly "part" or number consisted of three or four chapters, covering thirty-two pages of print, with two plates, and several pages of advertisements. It was issued in green paper covers and was published at a shilling, nominally on the first day, actually on the last day, of each month. This form of publication was chosen for *Pickwick* by Chapman and Hall, but Dickens found it so suitable that he adopted it for *Nicholas Nickleby, Martin Chuzzlewit, Dombey and Son, David Copperfield, Bleak House, Little Dorrit, Our Mutual Friend,* and *Edwin Drood.* Each of these novels . . . was planned for completion in nineteen monthly numbers, the last being a double number priced at two shillings, and containing, besides forty-eight pages of text and four plates, the title-page, frontispiece, preface, and other preliminaries. . . .

WRITING FOR SERIAL PUBLICATION

Although it might be supposed that Dickens would wish to complete a novel before permitting serial publication to begin, in fact he never wrote more than four or five numbers before the first was published, and by the middle of the novel he was rarely more than one number ahead of his readers. As might be expected, his practice differed at different stages of his career. . . .

The disadvantages of this method seem obvious. As [English novelist Anthony] Trollope remarked, "an artist should keep in his hand the power of fitting the beginning of his work to the end". And the difficulties seem equally great. Writing in serial involved maintaining two focuses. The design and purpose of the novel had to be kept constantly in view; but the writer had also to think in terms of the identity of the serial number, which would have to make its own impact and be judged as a unit. Incident and interest had therefore to be evenly spread, since "the writer . . . cannot afford to have many pages skipped out of the few which are to meet the reader's eye at the same time". Chapters must be balanced within a number in respect both of length and of effect. Each number must lead, if not to a climax, at least to a point of rest; and the rest between numbers is necessarily more extended than what the mere chapter divisions provide. The writer had also to bear in mind that his readers were constantly interrupted for prolonged periods, and that he must take this into account in his characterization and, to some extent, in his plotting. So early as the original preface to *Pickwick*, Dickens showed his recognition that not every story is suited to this type of publication.

Great as these difficulties were, they were felt to be worth overcoming. To the reader the system meant not merely eager expectation of the day which brought a fresh batch of green covers to the bookstall, but also the impression that the story was in the making from month to month. . . .

To the author it meant a larger public, but also a public more delicately responsive, who made their views known during the progress of a novel both by writing to him and by reducing or increasing their purchases. Through serial publication an author could recover something of the intimate relationship between story-teller and audience which existed [in the fourteenth century], in the ages of the sagas and of [Geoffrey] Chaucer; and for an author like Dickens, who was peculiarly susceptible to the influence of his readers, this intimate relationship outweighed the inherent disadvantages of the system.

LOGISTICAL PROBLEMS

Yet the disadvantages were none the less apparent, and they could be mastered only by more systematic planning than this impulsive man has been credited with. Publication day was the last day of each month, known in the trade as "magazine day". By that date Dickens had to plan and write the equivalent of thirty-two printed pages and to give his illustrator instructions for two engravings. The manuscript had to be sent to the printer in London. . . . Proofs were to be corrected and sent to press, and copies were to be sewn and distributed to booksellers. . . .

Frequently [Dickens] had to go straight from one number to the next; but often he could allow himself a few days' respite at the end of the month before beginning the next month's installment. Occasionally he resumed work as late as the seventh day. Thus he had about a fortnight [two weeks] for writing his three or four chapters.

He did not always complete his number before sending it to the printer. Sometimes it was delivered in batches with instructions for a proof to be forwarded to the illustrator. Hablôt Browne [an illustrator] was accustomed to work to orders. At best he had a proof to go upon; at worst his instructions were verbal. . . .

At a time when it might be expected that [Dickens's] energies would be fully expended upon writing his monthly installment, he must turn aside to create a scene in Browne's imagination, letting him into secrets, appropriately enough, which less privileged readers were left to guess, and speaking out straight on matters which in the novel he is content to hint at, but embodying here and there with little verbal change significant details from the manuscript before him. . . .

AT HIS WRITING DESK

Much is known about Dickens's habits at the desk. In the middle of his career, it was his normal custom to work in the mornings only from nine o'clock till two; but he was no clock-work performer. . . . As a young man he had been a fluent writer, able to drive himself to work all day; and the surviving sheets of manuscript of his earliest novels suggest a hand racing to keep pace with the mind's conceptions. . . . His letters to [John] Forster [Dickens's friend and biographer] written at this time suggest that eleven or twelve of these sheets, or "slips" as he called them, could be written in a day, or, at a push, as many as twenty. But at the height of his powers, he found more difficulty in satisfying himself, and from *Dombey and Son* onwards his manuscripts are characterized by frequent erasures and interlineations [writing between the lines]. . . . The different shades of ink which he used from time to time show that his habit was to correct as he wrote, sentence by sentence, and that though he subsequently read through the whole of his chapter, he rarely needed to make any later alteration.

The manuscripts he sent to press were these corrected first drafts. He never dictated to an amanuensis [one who received dictation], nor used a secretary to make a fair copy, and only in a few instances can we be sure that he took the trouble of rewriting a much-corrected slip. Indeed there was no time for what a modern printer regards as normal courtesy from his author; and as for dictation, it would only have hindered him, for he relied upon the knowledge that he had to fill about thirty slips in his normal handwriting to complete a monthly number. Thus Bradbury and Evans, his printers, had to make do with "copy" obscure enough to daunt the most experienced compositor. Not only was it written in a small hand with all too little space left between lines for the numerous interlineations, but the text was sprinkled with peculiar proper names.

Life into Art, Autobiography into Fiction

Fred Kaplan

Fred Kaplan, a Dickens scholar, taught English at Queens College and the Graduate Center (CUNY). He has edited the prestigious Norton Critical Edition of *Oliver Twist* and written a highly praised biography of Dickens, from which this excerpt is taken.

After writing many novels analyzing the suffering of the lower classes and the corruption of society, Dickens reached a stage in the 1840s when he felt the need to write about his own life in a fictionalized autobiography, a novel entitled *David Copperfield*. Critics have pointed out that Dickens provided a clue to his intention by giving the initials "DC" to David Copperfield, his alter ego and the first-person narrator of the novel; these were in fact his own initials, "CD," reversed. This novel afforded Dickens an opportunity to examine the unresolved family dynamics of his relations with his parents and siblings and to attempt to divest himself of traumatic childhood memories. At the same time, Dickens projected a fictionalized version of his marriage into the novel, aware as he was that his relationship with his wife was a troubled one. There were several other factors which impelled Dickens to fictionalized self-analysis—approaching middle age, his responsibilities as a paterfamilias (head of the household), and his prominence as a public figure.

When completing *David Copperfield*, Dickens experienced a powerful aftereffect that left him confused about "whether to laugh or to cry ... strangely divided ... between sorrow and joy." He felt that he had been turned inside out, his inner life

Fred Kaplan, *Dickens: A Biography*. London: Sceptre, 1989. Copyright © 1988 by Fred Kaplan. Reproduced by permission.

now visible, in partly disguised forms, in the shadowy world of ordinary daylight. The story he had written was so deeply personal that "no one can believe [it] in the reading, more than I have believed it in the writing." Having transformed his private memories and his emotional life into a public myth about himself, particularly his development from an abandoned child into a great popular artist surrounded by love and success, he felt the excitement both of exposure and catharsis [cleansing]. Exorcising the wounds of childhood and young adulthood, he also dramatized the unresolved problems of his personality and his marriage, anticipating the turmoil that was to come. Though energized by the process of writing, he was also exhausted. . . .

FICTIONAL TRANSFORMATION

In *David Copperfield* he re-created in mythic terms his relationship with his mother, his father, his siblings, particularly Fanny, and with his wife and his wife's sisters. The novel was more precious to him than his own children because the favorite child was himself. Soon after beginning, he confessed that he had stuck to that fictional name through the exploration of alternative titles because he had, even at the earliest stage, recognized that he was writing about himself. . . . When it came to his novels, the distinction between self and other was subordinated to the dramatization of the many varieties of the single self. Changing Charles Dickens into David Copperfield had the force both of unconscious reversal and of minimal autobiographical distancing. At the heart of the novel was a partly mediated version of himself that represented his effort to claim that he had come through, that all was well with him as he approached the age of forty.

There was much, though, that was troublesome. He had fatherhood with a vengeance, particularly difficult for someone who both embraced and rebelled against patriarchy. He had a superficially successful marriage that provided him with neither romance nor companionship. He had ostensibly left behind a childhood whose experiences and memories still galled him in the present. He had a future whose patterns promised to be similar to those he already knew, his opportunities for adventure limited by his personal and professional obligations, by the restraints of success, and by the pressure to keep earning at a high level. No longer a

young man, he assumed, becoming an honored public figure of prominence and distinction, a Victorianism that he
was not fully ready for and that the artist within him was uncomfortable with, perhaps even rebelled against. There were
the first visible signs of middle age. The mobility of his face
had now the counterpoint of some permanent lines. His lux-
uriant hair began to show a receding silky thinness. Having
been forced from an early age to look after himself, he now
had to look after others as well as to anticipate the trials of
middle age, though he had hardly had the pleasures of a real
childhood. Time and nature were re-creating him along
their own lines, and the social world that he had built as a
secure pleasure house contained more restraint than he had
anticipated. In fact, he had anticipated very little.

CHILDHOOD

From his adult perspective, he combined fiction and autobiography into an expression of the truth about his emotional
life at the end of the 1840s. Telling his own story, the artist-
writer, like the adult David Copperfield, imagines his own
birth, beginning with a prelapsarian [Edenic] fantasy of perfect harmony with his mother. [David's] father has died be-

*Charles Dickens, pictured above in his study at Gad's Hill Place,
explored the events of his own life in a fictionalized autobiography,* David Copperfield.

fore he is born, a convenient extermination of an ideal who is not given the opportunity to disappoint his son. John Dickens is distanced by being divided into two unsatisfactory father figures [in the novel], Murdstone and Micawber, neither of whom is David's real father. The boy's infantile idyll with his mother is soon shattered by her remarriage, an expression of her own infantilism, dependency, and ambivalent feeling for her son, who is shocked to discover that he alone cannot satisfy his mother's needs. Like Dombey, Murdstone represents Dickens' view of the father as an unfeeling mechanism of discipline whose life gains its shape and strength from restraining himself and others. Micawber radiates with the more subtly dangerous attractions of a father whose intentions are essentially loving but whose weaknesses undermine family stability. Micawber, though, is not David's father. David's father is safely dead. Though at great cost, his mother's second husband, Murdstone, is neutralized, and Micawber becomes the friend whom David can help, eventually off to Australia, where he is out of sight if not out of mind. A Falstaffian [riotous, like Falstaff, a Shakespearian character] figure, with innumerable touches of language and outlook derived from John Dickens, Micawber is neither allowed the power to hurt David nor disallowed the warmth of his basic benevolence.

David's mother dies under the heartless regimen [control] of her second husband, whose cruelty provides Dickens with a mechanism for making David an orphan. Just as Dickens sends Micawber to Australia, he sends David's mother to the grave. But the fictional mother that he buries, broken-hearted, is a counterimage of his feelings about his own. She is the mother that Dickens would have preferred to have had. An idealized representation of unselfish maternity, she is forced to desert her son from her first marriage, a hapless innocent caught in the web of Murdstone's sexual and social authority, without the strength to liberate herself except through the grave, to which she also takes her second son. Though he is Murdstone's progeny, David's "baby brother" is an image of his sense of loss and abandonment, the mother he hardly had, the sibling who came between them. "So I lost her. So I saw her afterwards, in my sleep at school—a silent presence near my bed—looking at me with the same intent face—holding up her baby in her arms." As an adult, [David] remarks that "if the funeral had

MOTHERLESS CHILDREN

Dickens's biographers repeatedly correlate the writer's own unhappy childhood experiences with the way that he depicted children in his fiction. In particular, Dickens's deep disappointment with his mother in his early years is generally regarded as the explanation of why so many of the children in Dickens's novels were deliberately made motherless by the author.

Barbara Charlesworth Gelpi, who taught English at Stanford University, goes even further, arguing that Dickens was compelled to show children without mothers because the alternative, to portray maternal neglect or mistreatment of their children, would have been unbearably painful to him and would have revived his own childhood memories of his mother to an unbearable extent.

Dickens' children are usually bereft [deprived] of their mothers through death, that absence being then no fault of the mothers. So Oliver Twist, Little Nell, the Dombey children, David Copperfield, Esther Summerson—all are motherless. As a novelist Dickens was thus able to take much though not all of the sting out of his portrayal of these mothers' inadequacy, but his own autobiographical sketch helps to explain why he took the mothers offstage. After Dickens' father was released from debtors' prison, he quarreled with the relative for whom Dickens worked at the blacking factory, and Dickens lost his job there. His mother went down the next day to try to get it back. [In Dickens's words, as quoted by John Forster in *The Life of Charles Dickens:*] "My father said, I should go back no more, and should go to school. I do not write resentfully or angrily: for I know how all these things have worked together to make me what I am: but I never afterwards forgot, I never shall forget, I never can forget, that my mother was warm for my being sent back."

Barbara Charlesworth Gelpi, "The Innocent I: Dickens's Influence on Victorian Autobiography," in *The Worlds of Victorian Fiction*, ed. Jerome H. Buckley, Harvard English Studies 6. Cambridge, MA: Harvard University Press, 1975, p. 64.

been yesterday, I could not recollect it better. . . . The mother who lay in the grave, was the mother of my infancy; the little creature in her arms, was myself, as I had once been, hushed for ever on her bosom." In his childhood and into his adult life, David is sustained by a "fanciful picture of my mother in her youth, before I came into the world. It always kept me company.". . .

YOUTH AND MATURITY

Using passages from the autobiographical fragment [given by Dickens to Forster, his biographer], Dickens propels David through a fictionalized version of his early school experiences and then into the infamous blacking factory in the form of a wine warehouse, to which Murdstone consigns him, supposedly to make his way in the world but really to degrade and humiliate him. Whereas Dickens *felt* like an orphan, David *is* one. David's vision of himself as a scholar and a gentleman, like Dickens', is tested by adversity. Unlike [Dickens], though, [David] becomes headboy, the culmination of a school career normal for the children of the privileged, and he looks "down on the line of boys below me with a condescending interest in such of them as bring to my mind the boy I was myself, when I first came there." Dickens also draws with autobiographical vividness on his vocational development, associating David with the law, with stenography, with Doctors' Commons, with parliamentary reporting, with writing short fiction, and then with becoming a famous novelist. The narrator-author, though, is never deflected from his intent to write a story of inward vocation, the story of the development of a wounded child whose good heart and happy progress have been impeded by lost and false parents, social distortions, mistakes of perception, and emotional inexperience. Reality is turned into fable, loss into blessing, trouble into convenience, weakness into strength, restlessness into energy, and emotional confusion into clarity by the gift of love.

Dickens's Social Philosophy in the Major Works of the 1850s

Allan Grant

The novels written by Dickens in the 1850s are acclaimed as some of his greatest works. Within just a few years, he wrote (and arranged to have published) *Bleak House, Hard Times,* and *Little Dorrit.* All three are scathing indictments of the injustice and corruption prevalent in Victorian England. During this period, Dickens and Thomas Carlyle, the eminent social historian, were good friends, alike both in their condemnation of British society and in their ceaseless efforts to persuade the public of the necessity for reform. It was in this decade too that Dickens wrote *A Tale of Two Cities*, a historical novel set in France at the time of the French Revolution (an event analyzed by Carlyle in his famous history of the French Revolution).

The biography of Dickens from which this excerpt is taken was written by Allan Grant, lecturer in English at London University. Grant records the extraordinary and ceaseless activities, both literary and nonliterary, which were undertaken by Dickens in the 1850s. In the course of this decade, he sold and bought several houses into which he moved with his family; he and his family traveled to the Continent several times for extended holidays lasting many months; he separated from his wife; he gave public readings of his works; he acted in theatrical performances, some of them for charity; he was involved in political activity, endorsing public outrage at the disastrous Crimean War of the mid-1850s; finally, he edited and even purchased journals, one of which published *Hard Times* as a serial novel.

Allan Grant, *A Preface to Dickens.* New York: Longman, 1984. Copyright © 1984 by Longman Group Ltd. Reproduced by permission.

In the middle of 1851 Dickens had to give up the Devonshire Terrace house. He bought Tavistock House, facing Tavistock Square in Bloomsbury, and turned to his next novel, *Bleak House*. If *David Copperfield* is a watershed in Dickens's career, then *Bleak House* is the first of the great series of late novels in the course of which he described an England corrupted by its obsolete institutions. In these novels, social misery is no longer laid at the door of evil individuals, but is felt to be part of the fabric of a rotten society. *Bleak House* uncovers the invisible threads that connect the most notorious decaying slums of the capital with the grand melancholy estates of the aristocracy. By this time Dickens had had a vast practical experience of attempts at social reform and private philanthropy, quite apart from what he had written as novelist and journalist. *Hard Times* followed within six months in *Household Words* in an attempt to rouse a flagging circulation, but again, Dickens had enormous difficulty in confining himself to the compression demanded by weekly instalments. The writing exhausted him and, for all the praise that has been expended on this short novel ([author and critic] John Ruskin thought it "in several respects the greatest he had written"), it does seem to me, despite the intelligence of its conception, to bear the marks of a strained imagination. This is not merely a matter of the mechanical and formal constraints so much as the tight rein put on the author's invention by the attempt to stay close to what is an identifiable idea: the incompatibility of, on the one hand, human life and imagination, and the tyranny of abstract, statistical theories of education and human worth on the other.

Despite the pressures and constraints of writing in weekly instalments, he took the family to Boulogne for the summer where he finished the novel in sight of the military preparations for the Crimean Campaign. He dedicated the finished work to Carlyle: "I know it contained nothing in which you do not think with me, for no man knows your books better than I."

THE CRIMEAN WAR

With the novel completed, he found himself utterly used up, "in a state of restlessness, impossible to be described—impossible to be imagined—wearing and tearing to be experienced." The Crimean War, which began in March 1854, had put a complete stop to any further attempts to reform Parliament and government, and by the winter the news of the catastrophic incompetence of the conduct of the campaign had become a national scandal. Of the army of fifty-four thousand sent to Russia only fourteen thousand were still alive and, of those, only five thousand fit for service. The government of Lord Aberdeen [George Hamilton-Gordon,] fell as a result of these appalling reports. Cholera accounted for the majority of the deaths and the same disease had swept through England during the year. Dickens's daughter Mary caught it in Boulogne, but recovered without any danger to the others in the house. *Household Words* took up the cause of reform; inveighing [denouncing] against the administration of Lord [Henry T.] Palmerston, "Twirling Weathercock" as Dickens called him, and supporting the Administrative Reform Association which was set up on the initiative of Austen Layard, the explorer of Nineveh [ancient Middle Eastern ruins] and a member of Parliament. At the same time, Dickens organised another round of private theatricals. This time it was to be *The Lighthouse*, a melodrama written by [playwright] Wilkie Collins. Its success in private encouraged the group of friends to give public performances for charity benefits on several occasions.

HOLIDAYS IN FRANCE

It was his preoccupation with public affairs, however, that directed him towards his next novel which he started in May 1854. Originally entitled *Nobody's Fault*, it became, in the writing, *Little Dorrit*, a sustained attack on the issue of the condition of England, the topic to which Carlyle addressed himself continuously during this period in a series of tracts and pamphlets. Monthly publication began in December, 1855. By then Dickens and his family were living in Paris in an apartment on the Champs Elysées where he was continuously entertained during the following eleven months by the leaders of intellectual and artistic life. What struck Dickens most forcibly about the Parisian scene were the high style of living and the importance to public life of the most famous artists, writers and publishers. There was, he felt, no such regard or respect paid to their counterparts in England. Furthermore, intellectual Paris took him seriously as an artist. Henri Taine wrote an article in the *Revue des Deux Mondes* placing him among the immortals of art. From Paris, and later from Boulogne where the family again spent a late summer, he made at least one business trip to London each month. He often had engagements to fulfil, public charity readings or speeches to give. It was while he was abroad that he bought Gad's Hill Place, a country house near Rochester, which was to be his final home in England. His father had shown him the house on a walk when he was still a small boy and had even said that he might live there if he grew up to become rich and famous. The other association with Gad's Hill is one which gave Dickens intense satisfaction. It was the scene of the memorable robbery enacted by Sir John Falstaff in Shakespeare's *Henry IV* Part 1. Dickens had Falstaff's words copied and framed for his visitors to read:

> But, my lads, to-morrow morning, by four o'clock,
> early at Gadshill! There are pilgrims going to
> Canterbury with rich offerings and traders riding to
> London with fat purses: I have vizards [masks] for you all
> you have horses for yourselves.

Dickens also noted that the growing railway system would connect him with the coastal towns of Kent and with London and so add to the convenience and value of his purchase.

THEATRICAL PRODUCTIONS

He was, however, still in the middle of writing *Little Dorrit* and, once again, absorbed in producing another play of Wilkie Collins's, *The Frozen Deep*, which he had re-written to a considerable extent. He also played the main part of the hero who sacrifices himself to save the life of his rival in love. Dickens's playing of the role had an extraordinary effect on audience and actors alike. A private performance was arranged for the Queen, Prince Albert and the King of the Belgians: also present was Dickens's long-staying house guest of that summer, Hans Christian Andersen, the Danish writer of fairy tales.

It was the sudden death of his friend, Douglas Jerrold, the playwright and humorist, that decided Dickens to give more readings of *The Christmas Carol* and performances of *The Frozen Deep* in public in order to raise money for Jerrold's family. Public performances meant professional actresses rather than his daughters and the wives of the company, and for the female roles he engaged two sisters [Maria and Ellen] and their mother, Mrs. [Frances] Ternan, a well-known actress. After performances in Manchester, the Jerrold fund had passed £2,000. Following these exertions, and after a dash north with [Wilkie] Collins for a short walking tour, Dickens was still restless and in great distress and wrote so to [John] Forster [his friend and biographer]. In the letter he confessed that he could no longer avoid the feeling that he and his wife [Catherine] were "not made for each other." Over the years she had been able to contribute increasingly little to his domestic life, though she had borne him eight children, and almost nothing to his public career. She had probably had little opportunity to do so whether or not she had the inclination. Even her part as mother had been taken over by Georgina [Catherine's sister] who had devoted her own life to the children and their father. What was also clear to Catherine by this time, although nothing was revealed publicly until 1934, was that Dickens had become infatuated with the younger Ternan sister, Ellen, during the final rehearsals in the Dickens's house for the public performances of *The Frozen Deep*. It was not the first time that she had grieved over her husband's relations with other women. In Genoa in 1848 he had given mesmeric treatment [hypnosis] to the wife of a local bank official, often in the middle of the night, ostensibly for depressive headaches and hallucinations. Over many years, as far as one can tell from the surviving correspondence, Dickens carried on apparently light-hearted affairs with a number of women. Even though his daughter Kate later wrote that her father never understood women, what is clear is that he was often attracted to them and, being the man he was, as often attracted them. Furthermore, Dickens had in recent years followed the lead of the younger sybaritic [pleasure-loving] Collins into a pursuit of pleasures more hedonistic than he had allowed himself hitherto. It was the intervention of Catherine's family, the Hogarths, that brought matters finally to a head and led to the break-up of the family. In June 1858 Dickens, in an astonishing and unattractive display, begged his readers' confidence in an article in *Household Words* headed "Personal". He wanted to put it also in *The Times* and *Punch*, an invitation which both journals refused. As the printers of *Punch* were also his publishers, he began to plan to free himself of them. At the same time he cut himself off from any friend who, for whatever reason, remained loyal to Catherine. She was swiftly settled in a separate house with Charlie [her son], while Georgina now took full charge of the household and the children. Charles and Catherine Dickens had been married twenty-two years; he was forty-six, she three years younger.

Public Readings and Journals

Before all was, as he wrote to Forster, "despairingly over" in June 1858, he had already begun the series of public readings from his works which now became an important feature of his life and travels and his main source of income. He felt that he needed something to do to take him out of his unhappiness and he also needed to earn more money in order to pay for Gad's Hill Place and the improvements he was continually proposing for the house. After an initial series in London, he took his readings on a tour of the principal cities of England and Scotland with such success that he was earning at the rate of £500 per week. Beginning with the *Carol* and *The Chimes*, he created sixteen readings in all from among short stories and scenes from the novels.

Back in London he completed his arrangements to break free of his publishers and return to Chapman and Hall. Refusing any compromise, Dickens forced Bradbury and Evans to sell to him at auction their portion of the stock of *Household Words* and advertised the last number of that magazine for 28 May, and the first of his new weekly magazine, *All the Year Round*, for April 1859. From the beginning the new venture carried *A Tale of Two Cities*, one of his most popular stories even though, as a novel, it is in many ways much inferior to his best writing. In the midst of everything else that occupied him or otherwise obstructed him in his private life, he had managed to get down to the writing in March after an appeal for background reading to Carlyle, author of what was at that time the best-known history of the French Revolution. Carlyle sent his friend two cartloads of books from the London Library. In addition to the weekly magazine instalments, the novel was published simultaneously in monthly parts in the green covers. It was the last novel on which Phiz [pseudonym used by Hablot Knight Browne] worked as illustrator. In June Dickens moved himself finally to Gad's Hill to finish writing the novel. The weather was hot and the "small portions drive me frantic; but I think the tale must have taken a strong hold". It did, and the new venture was even more profitable to him than *Household Words* had been. Forster turned "white with admiring approval" and Carlyle found the story "wonderful."

After a summer at Gad's Hill and an autumn reading tour, he tried and failed to persuade George Eliot [a female novelist] to write a serial for him. Collins's *The Woman in White* was a sensation, but the following serial failed to attract readers and so, in the next year he began, at a moment's notice it would seem, *Great Expectations* for the magazine. . . . He sold off Tavistock House and, at Gad's Hill, burned all his past correspondence, expressing the wish that all the letters he had ever written were also on the bonfire. He gave away his eldest daughter Kate in marriage to Collins's brother, a Pre-Raphaelite painter and writer whose work Dickens admired sufficiently to print occasional pieces by him. Allston Collins was seldom in good health and was twelve years older than his bride and Dickens had advised her against marrying him. He was absent from his oldest son's wedding in November, but was delighted a year later by the "unmitigated nonsense" of becoming a grandfather.

The Criminal and the Rebel

Edmund Wilson

Edmund Wilson, author of numerous works on literature, political ideology, and cultural studies, was one of the most distinguished twentieth-century American scholars. The following extract, taken from Wilson's classic long essay on Dickens, "The Two Scrooges," was first published in his seminal work *The Wound and the Bow*.

Wilson analyzes Dickens's creative imagination, arguing that a recurrent character-type used by Dickens in his fiction was that of the criminal, while the critical stance typically adopted by Dickens himself was that of the rebel. Wilson traces Dickens's fascination with the criminal mind in many novels, alluding to *Oliver Twist* which, surprisingly, he does not discuss. It should be noted, however, that among the melodramatic episodes portrayed in *Oliver Twist* are two graphic scenes—one in which the criminal, Bill Sikes, murders his lover, Nancy, followed by the scene in which Sikes is hanged. Biographers point out that in the latter years of Dickens's life, he gave public readings of his novels in which he returned to these scenes, dramatizing their violence on stage with such emotional intensity that, night after night, he drove his audience to the verge of mass hysteria. Indeed, many claim that the stress and strain of acting out these scenes actually shortened Dickens's life.

At the same time, *Oliver Twist*, like many of the other novels discussed by Edmund Wilson, is an expression of Dickens's rebellion—a protest against the privations and cruelty suffered by the poor in Victorian society.

Edmund Wilson, *The Wound and the Bow: Seven Studies in Literature*. London: W.H. Allen, 1952.

For the man of spirit whose childhood has been crushed by the cruelty of organized society, one of two attitudes is natural: that of the criminal or that of the rebel. Charles Dickens, in imagination, was to play the rôles of both, and to continue up to his death to put into them all that was most passionate in his feeling.

PRISONS AND PRISONERS

His interest in prisons and prisoners is evident from the very beginning. In his first book, *Sketches by Boz*, he tells how he used to gaze at Newgate with "mingled feelings of awe and respect"; and he sketches an imaginary picture of a condemned man's last night alive, which he is soon to elaborate in *Oliver Twist*. Almost the only passage in *American Notes* which shows any real readiness on Dickens' part to enter into the minds and feelings of the people among whom he is travelling is the fantasy in which he imagines the effects of a sentence of solitary confinement in a Philadelphia jail. He visited prisons wherever he went, and he later found this cruel system imitated in the jail at Lausanne. Dickens was very much gratified when the system was finally abandoned as the result of the prisoners' going mad just as he had predicted they would. He also wrote a great deal about executions. One of the vividest things in *Pictures from Italy* is a description of a guillotining; and one of the most impressive episodes in *Barnaby Rudge* is the narration—developed on a formidable scale—of the hanging of the leaders of the riots. In 1846, Dickens wrote letters to the press in protest against capital punishment for murderers, on the ground among other grounds that this created sympathy for the culprits; in 1849, after attending some executions in London with Forster, he started by writing to *The Times* an agitation which had the effect of getting public hangings abolished. Even in 1867, in the course of his second visit to America, "I have been tempted out," Dickens wrote . . . "at three in the morning to visit one of the large police station-houses, and was so fascinated by the study of a horrible photograph-book of thieves' portraits that I couldn't put it down."

His interest in the fate of prisoners thus went a good deal further than simple memories of the debtors' prison or notes of a court reporter. He identified himself readily with the thief, and even more readily with the murderer. The man of powerful will who finds himself opposed to society must, if he cannot upset it or if his impulse to do so is blocked, feel a compulsion to commit what society regards as one of the capital crimes against itself. With the anti-social heroes of Dostoevsky, this crime is usually murder or rape; with Dickens, it is usually murder. His obsession with murderers is attested by his topical pieces for *Household Words*; by his remarkable letter . . . on the performance of the French actor Lemaître in a play in which he impersonated a murderer; by his expedition, on his second visit to America, to the Cambridge Medical School for the purpose of going over the ground where Professor Webster had committed a murder in his laboratory and had continued to meet his pupils with parts of the body under the lid of his lecture-table. In Dickens' novels, this theme recurs with a probing of the psychology of the murderer which becomes ever more convincing and intimate. . . . We may . . . point out here that the crime and flight of Jonas Chuzzlewit [in *Martin Chuzzlewit*] already show a striking development beyond the cruder crime and flight of Sikes. The fantasies and fears of Jonas are really . . . the picture of a mind on the edge of insanity. What is valid and impressive in this episode is the insight into the consciousness of a man who has put himself outside human fellowship—the moment, for example, after the murder when Jonas is "not only fearful *for* himself but *of* himself" and half expects, when he returns to his bedroom, to find himself asleep in the bed.

BARNABY RUDGE

At times the two themes—the criminal and the rebel—are combined in a peculiar way. *Barnaby Rudge*—which from the point of view of Dickens' comedy and character-drawing is the least satisfactory of his early books—is, up to *Martin Chuzzlewit*, the most interesting from the point of view of his deeper artistic intentions. It is the only one of these earlier novels which is not more or less picaresque and, correspondingly, more or less of an improvisation (though there is a certain amount of organization discernible in that other sombre book, *Oliver Twist*); it was the only novel up to that time which Dickens had been planning and reflecting on for a long time before he wrote it: it is first mentioned in 1837, but was not written till 1841. Its immediate predecessor, *The Old Curiosity Shop*, had been simply an impromptu yarn, spun out—when Dickens discovered that the original scheme of *Master Humphrey's Clock* was not going over with his readers—from what was to have been merely a short story; but *Barnaby Rudge* was a deliberate attempt to find expression for the emotions and ideas that possessed him.

The ostensible subject of the novel is the anti-Catholic insurrection known as the "Gordon riots" which took place in London in 1780. But what is obviously in Dickens' mind is the Chartist agitation for universal suffrage and working-class representation in Parliament which, as a result of the industrial depression of those years, came to a crisis in 1840. In Manchester the cotton mills were idle, and the streets were full of threatening jobless men. In the summer of 1840 there was a strike of the whole north of England, which the authorities found it possible to put down only by firing into the working-class crowds; this was followed the next year by a brickmakers' strike, which ended in bloody riots. Now the immediate occasion for the Gordon riots had been a protest against a Bill which was to remove from the English Catholics such penalties and disabilities as the sentence of life imprisonment for priests who should educate children as Catholics and the disqualifications of Catholics from inheriting property; but the real causes behind the demonstration have always remained rather obscure. It seems to indicate an indignation more violent than it is possible to account for by mere anti-Catholic feeling that churches and houses should have been burnt wholesale, all the prisons of London broken open, and even the Bank of England attacked, and that the authorities should for several days have done so little to restrain the rioters; and it has been supposed that public impatience at the prolongation of the American War, with a general desire to get rid of George III, if not of the monarchy itself, must have contributed to the fury behind the uprising.

This obscurity, at any rate, allowed Dickens to handle the whole episode in an equivocal way. On the surface he reprobates Lord George Gordon and the rioters for their fanatical or brutal intolerance; but implicitly he is exploiting to the limit certain legitimate grievances of the people: the neglect of the lower classes by a cynical eighteenth-century aristocracy, and especially the penal laws which made innumerable minor offences punishable by death. The really important theme of the book—as Dickens shows in his preface, when he is discussing one of the actual occurrences on which the story is based—is the hanging under the Shop-lifting Act of a woman who has been dropped by her aristocratic lover and who has forged notes to provide for her child. This theme lies concealed, but it makes itself felt from beginning to end of the book. And as *Pickwick*, from the moment it gets really under way, heads by instinct and, as it were, unconsciously straight for the Fleet prison, so *Barnaby Rudge* is deliberately directed toward Newgate, where, as in *Pickwick* again, a group of characters will be brought together; and the principal climax of the story will be the orgiastic burning of the prison. This incident not only has nothing to do with the climax of the plot, it goes in spirit quite against the attitude which Dickens has begun by announcing. The satisfaction he obviously feels in demolishing the sinister old prison, which, rebuilt, had oppressed him in childhood, completely obliterates the effect of his right-minded references in his preface to "those shameful tumults", which "reflect indelible disgrace upon the time in which they occurred, and all who had act or part in them." In the end, the rioters are shot down and their supposed instigators hanged; but here Dickens' *parti pris* [bias] emerges plainly: "Those who suffered as rioters were, for the most part, the weakest, meanest and most miserable among them." The son of the woman hanged for stealing, who has been one of the most violent of the mob and whose fashionable father will do nothing to save him, goes to the scaffold with courage and dignity, cursing his father and "that black tree, of which I am the ripened fruit."

Dickens has here, under the stimulus of the Chartist agitation, tried to give his own emotions an outlet through an historical novel of insurrection.... Indeed, perhaps the best thing in the book is the creation that most runs away with the general scheme that Dickens has attempted. Dennis the hangman, although too macabre to be one of Dickens' most popular characters, is really one of his best comic inventions, and has more interesting symbolic implications than Barnaby Rudge himself. Dennis is a professional executioner, who has taken an active part in the revolt, apparently from simple motives of sadism. Knowing the unpopularity of the hangman, he makes an effort to keep his identity a secret; but he has found this rather difficult to do, because he sincerely loves his profession and cannot restrain himself from talking about it. When the mob invades Newgate, which Dennis knows so well, he directs the liberation of the prisoners; but in the end he slips away to the condemned cells, locks them against the mob and stands guard over the clamoring inmates, cracking them harshly over the knuckles when they reach their hands out over the doors. The condemned are his vested interest, which he cannot allow the rebels to touch. But the momentum of the mob forces the issue, breaks through and turns the criminals loose. When we next encounter Dennis, he is a stool pigeon, turning his former companions in to the police. But he is unable to buy immunity in this way; and he is finally hanged himself. Thus this hangman has a complex value: he is primarily a sadist who likes to kill. Yet he figures as a violator as well as a protector of prisons. In his rôle of insurgent, he attacks authority; in his rôle of hangman, makes it odious. Either way he represents on Dickens' part a blow at those institutions which the writer is pretending to endorse. There is not, except in a minor way, any other symbol of authority in the book.

Two Revolutionary Novels

The formula of *Barnaby Rudge* is more or less reproduced in the other two novels of Dickens that deal with revolutionary subjects—which, though they belong to later periods of Dickens' work, it is appropriate to consider here. In *Hard Times* (1854), he manages in much the same way to deal sympathetically with the working-class protest against intolerable industrial conditions at the same time that he lets himself out from supporting the trade-union movement. In order to be able to do this, he is obliged to resort to a special and rather implausible device. Stephen Blackpool, the honest old textile worker, who is made to argue the cause of the workers before the vulgar manufacturer Bounderby, refuses to join the union because he has promised the woman he loves that he will do nothing to get himself into trouble. He thus finds himself in the singular position of being both a victim of the blacklist and a scab [worker refusing to strike]. The trade-union leadership is represented only—although with a comic fidelity, recognizable even to-day, to a certain type of labour organizer—by an unscrupulous spell-binder whose single aim is to get hold of the workers' pennies. Old Stephen, wandering away to look for a job somewhere else, falls into a disused coal-pit which has already cost the lives of many miners, and thus becomes a martyr simultaneously to the employers and to the trade-union movement. In *A Tale of Two Cities* (1859), the moral of history is not judged as it is in *Barnaby Rudge*, but the conflict is made to seem of less immediate reality by locating it out of England. The French people, in Dickens' picture, have been given ample provocation for breaking loose in the French Revolution; but once in revolt, they are fiends and vandals. The vengeful Madame Defarge [who sits knitting, watching aristocrats being beheaded by guillotine] is a creature whom—as Dickens implies—one would not find in England, and she is worsted [outdone] by an Englishwoman. . . . There is in this book as in the other two—though less angrily expressed—a threat. If the British upper classes, Dickens seems to say, will not deal with the problem of providing for the health and education of the people, they will fall victims to the brutal mob. This mob Dickens both sympathizes with and fears.

Through the whole of his early period, Dickens appears to have regarded himself as a respectable middle-class man. If Sam Weller, for all his outspokenness, never oversteps his rôle of valet, Kit in *The Old Curiosity Shop* is a model of deference toward his betters who becomes even a little disgusting.

DICKENS IN AMERICA

When Dickens first visited America, in 1842, he seems to have had hopes of finding here something in the nature of that classless society which the foreign "fellow-travellers" of yesterday went to seek in the Soviet Union; but, for reasons both bad and good, Dickens was driven back by what he did find into the attitude of an English gentleman, who resented the American lack of ceremony, was annoyed by the American publicity, and was pretty well put to rout [utterly defeated] by the discomfort, the poverty and the tobacco-juice which he had braved on his trip to the West. Maladjusted to the hierarchy at home, he did not fit in in the United States even so well as he did in England: some of the Americans patronized him, and others were much too familiar. The mixed attitude . . . which was produced when his British ideas intervened to rein in the sympathy which he tended to feel for American innovations, is well indicated by the passage in *American Notes* in which he discusses the factory-girls of Lowell. These girls have pianos in their boarding-houses and subscribe to circulating libraries, and they publish a periodical. "How very preposterous!" the writer imagines an English reader exclaiming. "These things are above their station." But what is their station? asks Dickens. "It is their station to work," he answers. "And they *do* work. . . . For myself, I know no station in which, the occupation of to-day cheerfully done and the occupation of to-morrow cheerfully looked to, any one of these pursuits is not most humanizing and laudable. I know no station which is rendered more endurable to the person in it, or more safe to the person out of it, by having ignorance for its associate. I know no station which has a right to monopolize the means of mutual instruction, improvement and rational entertainment; or which has even continued to be a station very long after seeking to do so." But he remarks that "it is pleasant to find that many of [the] Tales [in the library] are of the Mills, and of those who work in them; that they inculcate habits of self-denial and contentment, and teach good doctrines of enlarged benevolence." The main theme of *Nicholas Nickleby* is the efforts of Nicholas and his sister to vindicate their position as gentlefolk.

THE POLITICAL NOVELS

But there is also another reason why these political novels of Dickens are unclear and unsatisfactory. Fundamentally, he was not interested in politics. As a reporter, he had seen a good deal of Parliament, and he had formed a contemptuous opinion of it which was never to change to the end of his life. The Eatanswill elections in *Pickwick* remain the type of political activity for Dickens; the seating of Mr. Veneering in Parliament in the last of his finished novels is hardly different. The point of view is stated satirically in Chapter XII of *Bleak House*, in which a governing-class group at a country house are made to discuss the fate of the country in terms of the political activities of Lord Coodle, Sir Thomas Doodle, the Duke of Foodle, the Right Honourable William Buffy, M.P., with his associates and opponents Cuffy, Duffy, Fuffy, etc., while their constituents are taken for granted as "a certain large number of supernumeraries, who are to be occasionally addressed, and relied upon for shouts and choruses, as on the theatrical stage." A little later (30th September, 1855), he expresses himself explicitly in the course of a letter to Forster: "I really am serious in thinking—and I have given as painful consideration to the subject as a man with children to live and suffer after him can honestly give to it—

that representative government is become altogether a failure with us, that the English gentilities and subserviences
render the people unfit for it, and that the whole thing has
broken down since that great seventeenth-century time, and
has no hope in it."

In his novels from beginning to end, Dickens is making
the same point always: that to the English governing classes
the people they govern are not real. It is one of the great purposes of Dickens to show you these human actualities who
figure for Parliament as strategical counters and for Political
Economy as statistics; who can as a rule appear only even in
histories in a generalized or idealized form. What does a
workhouse under the Poor Laws look like? What does it feel
like, taste like, smell like? How does the holder of a post in
the government look? How does he talk? what does he talk
about? how will he treat you? What is the aspect of the
British middle class at each of the various stages of its
progress? What are the good ones like and what are the bad
ones like? How do they affect you, not merely to meet at dinner, but to travel with, to work under, to live with? All these
things Dickens can tell us: It has been one of the principal
functions of the modern novel and drama to establish this
kind of record; but few writers have been able to do it with
any range at all extensive. None has surpassed Dickens.

No doubt this concrete way of looking at society may have
serious limitations. Dickens was sometimes actually stupid
about politics. His lack of interest in political tactics led him,
it has sometimes been claimed, to mistake the actual significance of the legislation he was so prompt to criticize. . . .
[Thomas] Macaulay complained that Dickens did not understand the Manchester school of utilitarian economics [use-
fulness as a guiding principle] which he criticized in *Hard
Times*. But Dickens' criticism does not pretend to be theoret-
ical: all he is undertaking to do is to tell us how practising
believers in Manchester utilitarianism behave and how their
families are likely to fare with them. His picture is strikingly
collaborated by the autobiography of John Stuart Mill, who
was brought up at the fountainhead of the school, in the
shadow of [Jeremy] Bentham [the leading utilitarian philoso-
pher] himself. In Mill, choked with learning from his childhood, overtrained on the logical side of the mind, and col-
lapsing into illogical despair when the lack began to make
itself felt of the elements his education had neglected, the

tragic moral of the system of Gradgrind is pointed with a sensational obviousness which would be regarded as exaggeration in Dickens.

DICKENS THE REBEL

This very distrust of politics, however, is a part of the rebellious aspect of Dickens. Dickens is almost invariably *against* institutions: in spite of his allegiance to Church and State, in spite of the lip-service he occasionally pays them, whenever he comes to deal with Parliament and its laws, the courts and the public officials, the creeds of Protestant dissenters and of Church of England alike, he makes them either ridiculous or cruel, or both at the same time.

In the work of Dickens' middle period—after the murder in *Martin Chuzzlewit*—the rebel bulks larger than the criminal.

Of all the great Victorian writers, he was probably the most antagonistic to the Victorian Age itself. He had grown up under the Regency and George IV; had been twenty-five at the accession of Victoria. His early novels are freshened by breezes from an England of coaching and village taverns, where the countryside lay just outside London; of an England where jokes and songs and hot brandy were always in order, where every City clerk aimed to dress finely and drink freely, to give an impression of openhandedness and gallantry. The young Dickens of the earliest preserved letters ... invites his friends to partake of "the rosy" [red wine]. ... From this point it is impossible, as it was impossible for Dickens, to foresee the full-length industrial town depicted in *Hard Times*. In that age the industrial-commercial civilization had not yet got to be the norm; it seemed a disease which had broken out in spots but which a sincere and cheerful treatment would cure.

CHAPTER 4

DICKENS'S MATURE YEARS

PEOPLE
WHO MADE
HISTORY

CHARLES DICKENS

Dickens's Condescending Attitude to Women

Michael Slater

In an age when an enlightened thinker such as John Stuart Mill was advocating rights for women and protesting what he termed "The Subjection of Women" (the title of his pamphlet published in 1869), Dickens was as conservative on this issue as most other members of Victorian society. It is indeed disturbing to note that, as sensitive as Dickens was to the suffering of victims of injustice, even to the extent of helping to establish a home for "fallen women" (prostitutes and female criminals released from prison), he could nonetheless be as complacent as most of his male contemporaries, content to keep women in what was considered to be their proper place.

Michael Slater, lecturer in English at London University and author of several books on Dickens, discusses this issue in his critical study, *Dickens and Women,* from which this excerpt is taken. He points out that Dickens was both conservative and conventional regarding the role of women, adopting the traditional view that a woman's proper place was in the home. He was prepared to find certain activities socially acceptable, such as writing novels and painting pictures, provided they could be practiced by women at home; but he drew the line at any activities requiring a public display, such as acting. Yet ironically he fell in love with an actress while experiencing marital difficulties and thereby destroyed his own marriage.

Whatever the oddities and idiosyncratic [peculiar] emphases in Dickens's presentation of virtuous woman in her domes-

Michael Slater, *Dickens and Women.* London: J.M. Dent & Sons Ltd., 1983. Copyright © 1983 by Michael Slater. Reproduced by permission.

tic role, what does overwhelmingly emerge from all his writings, both public and private, is a firm central conviction that the home is her proper natural element. Once woman ventures outside the family and seeks to do good on a large and public scale the result, Dickens felt, was bound to be unsatisfactory. Instead of guarding and maintaining the home as a place of healing restfulness and spiritual solace [comfort] for her menfolk toiling in the cut-throat world outside she brings the clamour and anxieties of that world, its "telegrams and anger", into the domestic sanctuary. In the essay "Sucking Pigs", . . . Dickens asks:

> . . . should we love our Julia better, if she were a Member of Parliament, a Parochial [local government] Guardian, a High Sheriff, a Grand Juror, or a woman distinguished for her able conduct in the chair? Do we not, on the contrary, rather seek in the society of our Julia, a haven of refuge from Members of Parliament, Parochial Guardians, High Sheriffs, Grand Jurors, and able chairmen? Is not the home-voice of our Julia as the song of a bird, after considerable bow-wowing out of doors?

NEGLECTING THE HOME

Mrs. Jellyby, of course, stands as Dickens's great example of woman betraying the home in this way, and it is not surprising that J.S. Mill should have been so angered by this part of *Bleak House* ("That creature Dickens . . . has the vulgar impudence in this thing to ridicule rights of women. It is done too in the very vulgarest way . . ."). She "devotes herself entirely to the public" and her preoccupation with "educating the natives of Borrioboola-Gha, on the left bank of the Niger" leads her to neglect her family. The house is dirty and uncomfortable, the servants unruly, the children survive as best they can, and the unfortunate husband sits despairingly in the kitchen with his head against the wall beseeching his eldest daughter never to have "a Mission". The clinching image comes in a description of the disorganized family dinner during which Mrs. Jellyby imperturbably [calmly] continues dealing with her business correspondence, receiving so many letters that Richard Carstone [a character in *Bleak House*], sitting by her, sees "four envelopes in the gravy at once". It is an unforgettable emblem of the domestic wrecked by the intrusion of the outer world.

Mrs. Jellyby is last heard of campaigning for "the rights of women to sit in Parliament". This for Dickens, as for his Queen (who was "most anxious to enlist every-one who can speak or write to join in checking this mad, wicked folly of 'Woman's Rights'"), and for the great majority of his fellow-citizens, represented the height of perverse female heroism, and the horror of the idea contributes strongly to the satire at the end of his spoof retelling of the story of Cinderella in 1853:

> Cinderella, being now a queen, applied herself to the govern-ment of the country on enlightened, liberal, and free princi-ples. All the people who ate anything she did not eat, or who drank anything she did not drink, were imprisoned for life. . . . She also threw open the right of voting, and of being elected to public offices, and of making the laws, to the whole of her sex; who thus came to be always gloriously occupied with public life and whom nobody dared to love.

(We can hear in this an echo of [poet Alfred, Lord] Ten-nyson's fear expressed in *The Princess* that "Sweet love" would be "slain" if women were to be made more like men.) Dickens was not unsympathetic towards the demand for ex-tending opportunities of employment for women, and he was prepared to support campaigns against specific legal and social injustices to women. But he never wavered from his conviction that female aspirations to participate in pub-lic life were . . . "a mad rebellion against the natural duties of their sex, and those characteristics known in the mass as womanliness". Dickens would have agreed with George Eliot [female novelist] in her definition of what actually con-stitutes this womanliness—"that exquisite type of gentle-ness, tenderness, possible maternity suffusing a woman's being with affectionateness, which makes what we mean by the feminine character". Involvement in public life would in-evitably, Dickens firmly believed, be destructive of this. Talking to Whitwell Elwin, editor of *The Quarterly Review*, in 1861 he said,

> The people who write books on the rights of women beg the question. They assume that if women usurped the functions of men it would be a clear gain,—so much added to their present merits. It never occurs to them that it would be destructive of what they have,—a total overthrow of everything in them which is winning and lovable. A male female is repulsive.

WOMEN NOVELISTS

One socially acceptable way in which certain women, at least, could reach out to a wider world than the domestic was through literature, especially the writing of novels. This was something which had Dickens's wholehearted sympathy. But he, like the Victorian literary establishment generally, would have made a sharp distinction between what George Eliot called "silly novels by lady novelists", the spate of so-called "fashionable novels", romantic twaddle about dukes and countesses and so on, produced by women like [Catherine Manners,] Lady Stepney (who, he commented, "could write quite as entertaining a book with the sole of her foot, as ever she did with her head") and the moving dramatizations of the emotional, moral and spiritual life of ordinary people created by the pens of such writers as Mrs. [Elizabeth] Gaskell or George Eliot herself.

By the mid-century there was a general recognition that women had made and were continuing to make an important and distinctive contribution to the contemporary novel. It was, however, a fundamental premise of such recognition that art, of any kind, produced by a woman would always be essentially different from—and ultimately inferior to—art produced by a man. Women's art, a young American journalist writing in *Blackwood's* had declared in 1824, would always be "less courageous, magnificent, and sublime" but it would be "more delicate, beautiful, and affecting... There would be more tenderness, more delicacy, more timidity in it." The heart and not the mind being held to "enshrine the priceless pearl of womanhood", as [writer Charles] Kingsley put it, it followed that women would shine most as writers when portraying feelings, nuances of emotion, the subtle fluctuations of personal relationships. Of all literary forms the novel was best suited to such matter. . . .

As we might expect, Dickens was less happy with women writers who dealt overtly with the passions rather than with the feelings unless, like Miss [Emily] Jolly in *The Wife's Story,* the writer showed passion in a woman as an evil force needing to be crushed. He read, [John] Forster tells us, very little of George Sand [French female novelist], despite her immense popularity in England at this time, and "had no very special liking" for such works of hers as he did know. . . .

WOMEN PAINTERS

Literary work, then, provided always that it took second place to whatever domestic responsibilities a woman might have, was quite reconcilable with Victorian public ideals about women. It is, as one novelist [Eliza Stephenson] remarked, in 1864, "of all employments the quietest. . . . There is nothing in it which need jar upon the retirement which every woman prizes so dearly". Another acceptable artistic activity for women was painting, though the number of those who, like Anne Brontë's Helen Huntington, [a character in Brontë's novel, *The Tenant of Wildfell Hall*], managed to gain an income from such work, must have been tiny in comparison with the number of earning female writers. . . .

No doubt [Dickens's] daughter Katey's growing seriousness about her art helped to influence him and it was sad that she did not begin to achieve recognition and success as an artist until after his death. . . . One of her paintings was accepted by the Royal Academy in 1877 and sold on the very first day it was exhibited. . . .

Dickens might indeed have rejoiced to see his favourite daughter beginning to make her way in the world as a painter but he was, we may recall, adamant that she should not embark on an acting career when, in 1870, she was contemplating this as a means of retrieving [rescuing] her and her husband's finances. For all the respect and adulation accorded to particular actresses in the mid-Victorian period the stage was not an acceptable career for a middle-class young lady—acceptable to her class and family, that is. Dickens's lifelong passion for the theatre brought him into friendly contact with many actresses (most famously and fatefully, of course, with the Ternan family) and his letters contain frequent appreciations of their work. Predictably, what he prized above all was an ability to project "womanly tenderness" or fresh girlish innocence from the stage. . . .

Actresses, unlike women novelists or women painters, had actually to practise their art in public and Dickens was torn between his pleasure in seeing aspects of his feminine ideal incarnated on the stage and his fervent concurrence with the age's belief that that ideal could only be realized in the home.

An Illicit Affair: Dickens and Ellen Ternan

Martin Fido

In the 1850s Dickens shocked many by his behavior, displaying what could only be regarded in Victorian society as ungentlemanly conduct. Although he had long been an ardent advocate of domestic harmony and happiness, he suddenly became mired in an ugly scandal: He demanded a separation from his wife amidst rumors of an extramarital affair with the actress Ellen Ternan. This episode is described in detail by Martin Fido in his biography, *Charles Dickens,* from which this extract is taken. Fido, a lecturer at universities in England, the United States, and the West Indies, has done extensive research on Dickens.

Fido shows that Dickens behaved in a surprisingly cruel and vulgar manner toward his wife Catherine (Kate), insisting upon conducting his quarrel with her in public. He issued declarations in the newspapers and demanded public and even printed apologies from his wife's relations, the Hogarths, whom he accused of slandering him. Even as he callously humiliated Catherine, he did his best to protect Ellen Ternan from scandal, praising the actress effusively but keeping her name out of the newspapers. As a result of the scandal, Dickens narrowly escaped public censure, which would certainly have damaged his reputation and adversely affected the sale of his writings.

There is a strange air of romantic fantasy about Dickens' passion for Ellen Ternan in 1857. "I wish I had been born in the days of Ogres and Dragon-guarded Castles", he wrote to a friend while he was on the *Lazy Tour* holiday with [Wilkie] Collins. "I wish an Ogre with seven heads (and no particu-

Martin Fido, *Charles Dickens.* London: Hamlyn, 1985. Copyright © 1970 by The Hamlyn Publishing Group Ltd. Reproduced by permission.

lar evidence of brains in the whole of them) had taken the Princess whom I adore—you have no idea how intensely I love her!—to this stronghold on the top of a high series of mountains, and there tied her up by the hair. Nothing would suit me half as well this day, as climbing after her, sword in hand, and either winning her or being killed.—*There's* a frame of mind for you, in 1857." And yet he took no advantage of the opportunity he had to prolong his stay at Doncaster for one day in order to watch the Ternan family's benefit performance at the theatre. His love for Ellen was so strongly based on his belief in her immaculate innocence and purity that he seems to have been afraid of sullying it by any overt approach. Instead, he eased his feelings by writing to his friends of her perfection, and ordered a bracelet for Ellen, just as he always ordered presents for actors and actresses who had worked with his amateur company.

DICKENS AND HIS WIFE QUARREL

Then disaster fell. The jeweller sent the bracelet to Tavistock House [Dickens's residence] by mistake, and it fell into Kate's hands. Added to Charles' withdrawal from her bedroom this was too much! She reproached and upbraided her husband, who in turn was outraged that such vile aspersions should be cast on his idealised love. In the recriminations which followed Kate soon lost her position of injured strength as Charles accused her of dirty-minded and malicious slander, and demanded that she publicly proclaim her belief in Ellen's innocence by paying the little actress a visit. Katey [Dickens's daughter] overheard sobbing in her mother's bedroom and went in, to be told of this unreasonable order. "You shall not go", cried Katey, stamping her foot. But Kate lacked the strength to resist her husband's imperious command and she went.

Nevertheless it was clear that breaking point had been reached. Mrs. Hogarth [Kate's mother] and Kate's youngest sister Helen, who had never really liked Charles, were understandably appalled by the humiliation imposed on her. It was they who suggested to her that she should ask for a separation.

SEPARATION

If they hoped that this would bring Dickens to his senses they made a grave miscalculation. He leaped at the proposal and immediately opened negotiations to decide on the details. At

Kate's request Mark Lemon generously acted for her while [John] Forster represented Dickens. These two [family friends] considered a variety of proposals: perhaps Kate could continue to act as hostess when Charles entertained and appear with him in public life while actually living separately? Or maybe the two could shuttle between Gad's Hill and Tavistock House, neither ever living in the same place at the same time? Kate rejected both these ideas, which would obviously have been inconvenient as well as undignified. The final agreement was that she should move to a little house on the edge of Camden Town with an income of six hundred pounds a year from Charles and with Charley [her son] as her companion. This did not mean that he would be her partisan: "Don't suppose", he pleaded with his father, "that in making my choice, I was actuated by any preference for my mother to you. God knows I love you dearly, and it will be a hard day for me when I have to part from you and the girls." No wonder poor Kate now passed whole days in weeping.

While the negotiations dragged on into 1858 Dickens moved into a small apartment at the *Household Words* office from which he wrote desperately to friends who deplored his conduct. Katey was to call her father "a wicked man—a very wicked man", in his treatment of her mother, and this hardly seems too strong a description of the man who could deliberately blacken his faithful and long-suffering wife's character, and tell all her remaining friends that she had been and still was a cold and unloving mother.

"Mary and Katey'" [Dickens's daughters], he told Miss Coutts [a friend of Dickens], "harden into stone figures of girls when they can be got to go near her, and have their hearts shut up in her presence as if they were closed by some horrid spring. No-one can understand this but Georgina [Kate's sister], who has seen it grow from year to year, and who is the best, the most unselfish, and most devoted of human Creatures. [Kate's] sister Mary, who died suddenly and who lived with us before her, understood it as well in the first month of our marriage. It is her misery to live in some fatal atmosphere which slays everyone to whom she should be dearest." The children confirmed that by the eighteen-fifties Kate's depression made her remote and inaccessible. But the suggestion that Mary Hogarth had ever found her sister unloving can only be regarded as a blatant lie. That Dickens should utter it with such passionate conviction gives some

DICKENS AND MARRIAGE

Harry Levin, professor of comparative literature at Harvard University and author of highly acclaimed works of literary criticism, finds an anomaly (a contradiction) in the Victorian public's view of Dickens. The failure of his own marriage and the unhappy marriages repeatedly depicted in his novels suggest that Dickens had a negative attitude to marriage. Nonetheless, as Levin points out, Dickens had the reputation of being "the family man" par excellence (above all others), and his novels were widely regarded as celebrating the joys of home and hearth.

Child of a once-broken home, Dickens went on to break up his own home, to be separated from his wife under circumstances of muted scandal. Celebrant of households and hearthsides and all the familial virtues, he depicted [in his novels] a sequence of marriages which fall surprisingly short of happiness more often than not—from the harsh antagonism of the Dombeys to the bittersweet union of David and Dora, not to mention a lumbering procession of henpecked husbands, ill-used wives, and comic mothers-in-law. Though adulteries are relatively few and far between, the suspicion frequently arises. . . .

Yet we continue to think of Dickens as preeminently the family man among novelists, and he supports this assumption by the number and the variety of *ménages* [households] he has exhibited, for better or for worse. The ideal was not less appealing to him because he felt compelled to show it so imperfectly realized, and the hopes of marital arrangement spring eternal in his happy endings.

Harry Levin, "The Uncles of Dickens," in *The Worlds of Victorian Fiction*, ed. Jerome H. Buckley. Harvard English Studies 6. Cambridge, MA: Harvard University Press, 1975, pp. 2–3.

indication of the misery he suffered—Katey said he was like a madman—while the fantasy of his love life destroyed the remaining peace of his family life.

THE RELATIONS GOSSIP

Just as the negotiations were almost complete a report reached Dickens' ears which led him to threaten cutting Kate off without a penny. Mrs. Hogarth and Helen had been explaining the separation to their friends as the result of Dickens' adultery. The fair name of Ellen Ternan was being publicly besmirched; and in a violent fury Dickens demanded that this claim be retracted. The gossips seemed to have been unconvinced by Dickens' vehement declarations of innocence; matters were at a standstill for a fortnight before the Hogarths could be persuaded to put their names to a document declaring that "we now disbelieve such statements. We know that they are not believed by Mrs. Dickens, and we pledge ourselves on all occasions to contradict them as entirely destitute of foundation." With this weapon in his hands Dickens carried his campaign for the proclamation of Ellen's virtue into the press. He drew up a statement of his own claiming that "some domestic trouble of long standing of a sacredly private nature" had been made "the occasion of misrepresentations, most grossly false, most monstrous and most cruel, involving not only me, but innocent persons dear to my heart, and innocent persons of whom I have no knowledge, if indeed they have any existence."

"Innocent persons" rather than "an innocent person" was used because slander had touched Georgina as well as Ellen. Georgina admired her brother-in-law and had no prospect of a career or security outside his house. She believed that she was doing useful work as his housekeeper and to her mother's amazement she refused to go into exile with Kate. Although her action went some way to convince a few people that Dickens' honour must be as bright as he claimed, others gloated over the possibility that Kate's own sister might be the disruptive mistress who had led to the separation. Such a liaison would have been incestuous both in law and in general opinion at the time, so that Dickens may have felt compelled to take public steps to clear the name of the sister-in-law who had courageously accepted an equivocal position on his behalf. "I most solemnly declare", he concluded his statement, "that all the lately whispered rumours touching the trouble at which I have glanced, are abominably false. And that whosoever repeats one of them after this denial will lie as wilfully and as foully as it is possible for any false witness to lie before Heaven and earth."

Newspaper Declarations

Forster sensibly told him that he could not possibly publish such a statement. Mark Lemon categorically refused to print it in *Punch*. Dickens agreed to abide by the decision of the editor of the *Times* who foolishly told him to go ahead and send it to the newspapers. And so a totally private matter, which might have been the substance of a little gossip in literary circles, was thrown open to the public.

Of course Dickens' statement made things worse rather than better. It was so vaguely worded that many readers had no idea what it was they were being told. Across the Atlantic Dickens' friends were perturbed by the garbled stories which reached them. In the silliest action of his career Dickens wrote another statement, a fuller and more elaborate one which was to be circulated privately among those of his distant acquaintances who were still dissatisfied. This found its way into the press, and what had formerly been known mysteriously as "some domestic trouble", was now generally revealed as a complete marital breakdown and separation. Worse still, this letter, which should never have been printed, made specific charges against Kate. "In the manly consideration towards Mrs. Dickens which I owe my wife", Dickens had written, "I will merely remark that the peculiarity of her character has thrown all the children on someone else.'" Helen and Mrs. Hogarth became "two wicked persons who should have spoken very differently of me, in consideration of earned respect and gratitude". Ellen's name was still concealed. She became "a young lady for whom I have great attachment and regard. Upon my soul and honour there is not on this earth a more virtuous and spotless creature than that young lady. I know her to be innocent and pure and as good as my own dear daughters. I will not repeat her name—I honor it too much."

PUBLIC SHOCK

This was a bombshell for the thousands of readers who saw Dickens as the laureate of hearth and home, the philosopher of Christmas who had persuaded Victorian England that family ties and cosy domestic junketings [outings] were among the highest blessings to be found in a Christian nation. The newspapers observed that it was a grave mistake for Dickens to tell readers "how little, after all, he thinks of the marriage tie". The heavy blame thrown on Kate was rightly castigated in the press: "This favourite of the public informs some hundreds of thousands of readers that the wife whom he was vowed to love and cherish had utterly failed to discharge the duties of a mother; and he further hints that her mind is disordered. If this is manly consideration, we should like to be favoured with a definition of unmanly selfishness and heartlessness." Nor did the protestations of innocence cut much ice. . . . It was with some trepidation that Forster watched the sales of the new journal *All the Year Round* for signs that self-created scandal might have shaken Dickens' popularity.

It was a relief to everyone that it had not—it would have been of no advantage to Kate to watch her husband's earning power dry up as she remained dependent on him.

Kate received general credit for her dignified silence. This was probably less a matter of considered policy than the dictate of her inactive temperament. For a short time Charley's presence and sympathy was a consolation to her, but soon he too had left her, as business called him to the Far East. She was brutally excluded from the remainder of her husband's life; she was not a guest at Katey's wedding, and she received the coolest acknowledgements to her letter of sympathy when Walter's [a son's] death in India was reported. She continued to read Charles' novels as they came out, and she clung hopelessly to her letters which, as she said, would show the world that he had indeed loved her once.

Charles was now free of Kate's presence, though there was no question of his marrying Ellen. Divorce had never entered his mind, either because this would have been a move which might seriously have damaged his sales, or because, like the majority of middle-class English men at the time, he did not approve of it.

No Divorce

Furthermore, he had no grounds for divorcing Kate (adultery was the only cause for which a wife might be divorced and Kate had been unquestionably faithful) and although she could possibly have accused him of cruelty or desertion, he was not a man who would meekly accept the role of guilty party when he believed himself totally innocent, even with an expedient end in view.

So for the rest of his life Dickens was without a wife. Georgina, whose domestic virtues had been celebrated in the pair of household heroines of his middle novels—Agnes in *David Copperfield* and Esther Summerson in *Bleak House*—became his housekeeper and oversaw the upbringing of the youngest children, Harry and Plorn. For some time Dickens kept a discreet fatherly eye on Ellen. Her elder sister Fanny married his friend Tom Trollope, brother of the novelist, and

Dickens, who had probably known the family for a considerable period of time, advised Mrs. [Frances] Ternan on the education and careers of her daughters. At the end of 1858 Ellen and her younger sister Fanny were living in lodgings in Berners Street off Oxford Street, and here Dickens helped them when an officious policeman called to enquire about the two young girls. Whether the constable suspected them of being in moral danger, living alone, or whether, as Dickens suspected, he had been bribed by a libidinous "swell" to establish contact with these supposedly "loose" actresses, cannot now be determined. But Dickens made a complaint to Scotland Yard on their behalf (it was the only occasion on which he criticised the police), and it must have been some years before Ellen actually became his mistress.

Dickens's Love of the Theater

Emlyn Williams

Emlyn Williams, eminent author and playwright, is internationally renowned for his dramatic stage readings of Dickens's novels. Williams's involvement in the theater seems to have given him special insight into Dickens's love of the theater, as is shown in the article from which this excerpt is taken.

Williams argues that, in another era, Dickens might well have had a career in the theater, whether as an actor or as a playwright. One of the reasons that he did not do so in his own time was the poor quality of the Victorian theater, which offered little scope for the development of his genius. Characters in plays of the time were stereotyped, and the audience expected little but vulgar spectacle on the stage. Thus, although Dickens was strongly attracted to the theater, he turned instead to writing novels. Yet his love of the dramatic and the theatrical as well as his desire to perform before an audience finally found expression when he began giving public readings of his novels. These became so popular and well attended that they can be regarded as providing a second career for Dickens. They had the added advantage of enabling him to earn extra money, which was constantly required by him to support his large family.

Why, if Dickens had the theatre so much in his blood that he was determined to be involved in "theatricals" as often as possible—why did he not train his magic pen to write for the theatre? One automatically discounts his frivolous potboiling contributions to the party spirit—*The Strange Gentleman* and such charadelike burlesque [a form of low comedy] improvisations as *O'Thello*—why did he never sit down and write, out of his own head, "a Play, by Charles Dickens"?

Emlyn Williams, "Dickens and the Theater," *Charles Dickens 1812–1870: A Centenary Volume*, edited by E.W.F. Tomlin. London: Weidenfeld and Nicolson, 1969. Copyright © 1969 by George Weidenfeld and Nicolson Limited. Reproduced by permission.

He never did, even when circumstances would seem to be turning his mind that way. It is on record—in his first preface to *A Tale of Two Cities*—that while he was playing in the [Wilkie] Collins drama *The Frozen Deep*, he "conceived the main idea of this story. A strong desire was upon me then to embody it in my own person." In other words, he had the idea of a play with Sydney Carton [character from *A Tale of Two Cities*] as the central character. But he never wrote it; it became another novel. A great one, but the play might have been great too. Why did he not?

THEATRE IN DICKENS'S TIME

The answer is simple: the play, written in London in the year 1857, could not have been great. Dickens was one of those men of genius who, however powerfully urged on by that genius, have yet to be—at some point—thwarted by the character of the age into which they have been born. He had, at all costs, to express himself dramatically: but the medium he would choose for that expression must perforce allow him to be true to himself, to give scope for sweeping eloquence, imaginative humour, chilling morbidity—all the unique qualities we know. And instinctively he knew, without even wondering about it, that writing for the theatre of his day could never give vent to all he was bursting to give.

The first three-quarters of the nineteenth century constituted the feeblest era of the British theatre: so feeble, indeed, as to be moribund [near death]. The official stages of Covent Garden and Drury Lane offered a series of classics of varying quality, interspersed with "new" plays which were already musty, being painstakingly stilted imitations of those classics. As for the free-lance theatres, they found themselves given over to a pit dominated by mindless gaping sightseers as opposed to playgoers; and intelligent people constantly expressed their puzzlement that they themselves, who demanded the highest standards in the books they read, would settle into a box cheerfully accepting beforehand the fact that they were about to witness an inept and vulgar spectacle not above the intelligence of a prurient [prying] potman in Long Acre.

LOW STANDARDS

It seemed to occur to nobody that the current theatre ought to aim at the same high standards as current literature. Even the most gifted authors, faced with the chance to make money by creating a piece for a London playhouse, were observed deliberately to lower their sights and write down to their putative [supposed] public: an attitude which led to such successful rubbish as [Edward] Bulwer-Lytton's *The Lady of Lyons,* and caused Douglas Jerrold, a gifted and witty man, to perpetrate such fashionable stuff as a farrago [mixture] of sentimentality called *Black-eyed Susan,* and to allow his *Rent Day*—which could have been as formidable and bold a work as *Hard Times*—to disintegrate into facile twaddle. Theatres were so vast that not only was it pretty impossible for the players to display subtlety of expression and gesture, there was no place either for detailed characterization in the writing. The *dramatis personae* [characters] of plays were as stereotyped as those of any medieval mystery: the hero was white of heart—brave, noble, chivalrous, a saint—and the villain black [of heart]: snarling, cruel, treacherous, a devil. The heroine was a simpering symbol of purity, the farmer simple, slow and endearing, the lawyer fawning and unscrupulous—strokes bold but meaningless.

Melodrama, farce, comic opera, operetta, burletta—burletta, operetta, comic opera, farce, melodrama [forms of light or comic entertainment in the theater]: the nomenclature [list of names] recurs with maddening regularity, and most presentations plagiarized one from the other. No, the theatre of his time and place was not good enough for Charles Dickens the writer. It is tantalizing to guess, if he had been born a hundred years later, what his position would be in the present-day theatre. I would wager it would be that of the major British playwright.

An Idea Is Born

"Nature intended me," said Dickens once to Bulwer-Lytton, "for the lessee of a National Theatre. Have pen and ink spoiled an actor-manager?" And to Mrs. Cowden Clarke, who had acted with him in *The Merry Wives of Windsor,* he declared just as plaintively, "I should like to be going all over the country and acting everywhere. There is nothing in the world equal to seeing the house rise at you. . . . One sea of delighted faces, one hurrah of applause. . . ." As the endless grindstone labour at his desk gave painful monthly birth to one masterpiece after another, the letters of appreciation were warm to the touch, as were the hand-clasps of strangers who stopped him in the street. But after all that work, it did not seem enough. He wanted much more. "A sea of delighted faces. . . ."

On 3 November 1844, in Genoa, he leaned back from his desk with a sigh of relief: yet another finished. *The Chimes.* To the printer as usual. But first . . .

He had an idea. That he would ask his mentor John Forster to invite a few close friends one evening to Forster's house in Lincoln's Inn Fields, where the author would read aloud to them his latest work.

Just to see.

Dickens can have had little idea what seed would now be planted, or of the tree into which the seed was to grow. But something was impelling him, even if he did not fully understand its gist—driving hard enough to persuade him to leave his wife and family behind in Italy, make a hair-raising winter journey over the Alps by sledge, return to London, and arrange the "little party, Monday December 2 at 6.30". Ten male friends, all distinguished men, including [Thomas] Carlyle, Douglas Jerrold and [Daniel] Maclise, who made a sketch of a scene he cannot have known would be of historic interest. It can only have seemed, beforehand, the harmless indulging of a popular author in an eccentric whim.

"High up in the steeple of an old church, far above the light and murmur of the town, and far below the clouds that shadow it, dwelt the Chimes I speak of . . ." [Extract from Dickens's Christmas book *The Chimes*]. For years to come, the sitting-rooms of a thousand English-speaking homes were to vibrate with Dickens's words as one member of the family read aloud to the assembled rest, who sat absorbed to hear—to see, almost—the words spring into new life. A *speaking* life. Imagine, then, the thrill of hearing those words come from the lips of their creator. ". . . Had Trotty dreamed? Are his joys and sorrows but a dream, himself a dream? The teller of this tale a dreamer, waking but now? . . . So may the New Year be a happy one to you, happy to many more whose happiness depends on you!" For Dickens's friends it was an experience, but for him it meant far more. A blessed release, from what he called "an unspeakable restless something".

Back through the snow to his family and the inevitable desk. He may have harked wistfully back to the ten rapt [absorbed, carried away] faces—hardly enough to form a sea, but rapt—but any stirring of any sort of plan, however vague, stayed well in the back of his mind.

FIRST PUBLIC READINGS

By 1846, it was becoming increasingly clear to the most successful novelist of his day, extravagant and encumbered with family, that he could hardly hope to extricate himself from financial cares by his pen alone. He was by now bold enough to write to Forster, in black and white, "I was thinking that a great deal of money might possibly be made by one's having readings of one's own books." Forster, conventional to a degree, dismissed the idea as unseemly: for a man in Dickens's exalted position, it savoured of literary prostitution. The subject was dropped. It took seven years for it to come up again—seven years of monthly part after monthly part—but come up again it did, as it had to do. In 1853, Dickens broached the matter in a craftily worded way—"Surely there could be no indignity in reading aloud publicly for a worthy charitable cause, *taking no remuneration* [pay]? Where would be the harm?" Forster, indeed, could not find any, though he would have been glad to; and on the evening of 27 December 1853, in Birmingham Town Hall, in aid of the Birmingham and Midland Institute, Dickens—aged forty-one—gave his first public reading from his own works: *A Christmas Carol.* He faced an audience of two thousand people. Two evenings later, *The Cricket on the Hearth.* Another two thousand. The "sea of faces" at last.

A SECOND CAREER

In December of the following year, 1854, after intense concentration on the grim *Hard Times,* Dickens celebrated with a second "bout" of benefit readings of the *Carol,* at Sherborne, Reading and Bradford [towns in Britain]. At Bradford Town Hall the crowd was so great that two rows of seats had to be arranged on the platform, behind Dickens: success could go no further, and the future could not be ignored, not by Forster or anybody else. A new career was looming up, a second one that could be infinitely exciting: the chariot of success would gallop the heavens harnessed not to one golden steed, but to two. It would take time—several years—but it would be done.

There was the occasional charity performance, as if to keep his hand in periodically—a sort of annual letting-off of steam. 4 October 1855, in Folkestone, the *Christmas Carol,* in aid of a local educational project; December, the *Carol* again at Peterborough and Sheffield [towns in Britain], in aid of their re-

A scene from A Christmas Carol, *one of the many novels from which Dickens read in his very popular public readings.*

spective Mechanics' Institutes; 31 July 1857, the *Carol*, in Manchester, in aid of a fund to help [the minor playwright] Douglas Jerrold's widow, followed in the next months by two performances of Wilkie Collins's play *The Frozen Deep* in the same cause, at the Free Trade Hall in the same city.

In this Dickens played a juicy leading role, but after the *Carol* less than a month before, it is not hard to imagine his feelings. It was one thing to appear in an efficient but essentially superficial melodrama, on a stage cluttered up with scenery and surrounded by actors and actresses of varying merit, several unable to cope with the acoustics of a vast auditorium—and another thing to stand alone on a bare stage, communing with an absorbed audience by means of magic words created, for all time, by himself and by none other. Frustrating . . .

But he had made a great success in the play—Wilkie Collins wrote that "he literally electrified the audience"—and these performances, solo and accompanied, were followed by a wretched reaction: bouts of depression which caused him to write to Collins, "In grim despair and wretchedness . . . I want to escape from myself. Anywhere—take any tour—see anything . . ." Then *Little Dorrit* [Dickens's current novel], engaged all his attention.

THE FINANCIAL MOTIVE

1858 was the decisive year. Agreeing to give one night of the *Carol* for the London Hospital for Sick Children, he again brought up to Forster the idea of giving public readings for his own financial benefit. Gad's Hill [Dickens's home], he insisted, had to be paid for. And there were personal problems of the most pressing kind, which he felt could be eased only by this solution. "I must do *something*," he wrote to Forster, "or I shall wear my heart away."

Finally Forster—muttering "cheap-jack"—grudgingly agreed. The charity reading at St Martin's Hall was to be followed by a series of sixteen nights "for his own profit".

From the moment the project was mooted [raised for discussion], success was assured: the charity performance was sold out, people booked immediately for the series, and the charity audience themselves flocked to rebook. It was a tide neither Canute [British king who thought he could stop the waves] nor Forster could have stemmed. In the twelve years between 1858 and the last reading, in London, on 15 March 1870, three months before his death ("From these garish lights I now vanish for evermore, with a heartfelt farewell . . .") he was constantly, while writing, going on a reading tour or planning one.

And 1867 saw a tour of the eastern United States which

was sensational. There were 423 (paid) readings in all, bringing in an estimated total income of £45,000 (then, of course, a staggering sum) which amounted to more than half the total value of his estate at his death. It had been a momentous decision.

Authors have read aloud in public before Dickens, and since—[William Makepeace] Thackeray, Mark Twain—but the Dickens phenomenon is unique.

An American Reading Tour

Norman and Jeanne MacKenzie

Dickens visited the United States twice, once in 1842
and again in 1867. His first visit was marred by his
angry outbursts in which he repeatedly and publicly
accused American publishers of violating the international copyright of his books, thereby infringing
upon his rights as author and depriving him of earn-
ings to which he was entitled. His accusations of-
fended American publishers and newspaper editors,
resulting in mutual hostility and acrimony.

Dickens's second trip to the United States began in
late 1867 and continued until 1868. This trip is described in detail by Norman MacKenzie, a lecturer at
Sussex University, and his wife Jeanne, in their well-
known biography, *Dickens: A Life*, from which the
following except is taken. The authors show that
Dickens's second tour of America was undertaken
primarily to earn money needed for his expenses in
England. Dickens scheduled a series of public readings of his novels, like those he had been giving in
England for many years. His tour proved to be a re-
sounding success financially and in other ways as
well. He was overwhelmed by the generosity of the
Americans in not bearing him any ill will for the
quarrels provoked by him on his previous visit in
1842. He was thrilled by their enthusiastic response
to his readings and by their thunderous applause.
Although he was aware that his international copyright was still being infringed, he decided to over-
look this issue since he had earned so much money
on the current tour.

While Dickens fretted, anxious to get to work, [George] Dolby
[his assistant] was busy with preparations. Despite the freez-

ing weather there had been day-long queues for tickets and the opening set of readings [in Boston] was sold out more than two weeks in advance. The eager Americans, Dickens wrote to his son Charley before the first performance, had little idea what to expect; "as they are accustomed to mere readings out of a book, I am inclined to think that the excitement will increase when I shall have begun".

For the first night Dickens chose the most popular of all his readings, giving *A Christmas Carol* and then the trial scene from *Pickwick.* He was greeted with deafening cheers when he walked on the stage; then after a moment's silence as he stood before his desk he began to read the familiar lines. "Success last night beyond description or exaggeration," Dickens wrote next day to Charley. "The whole city is quite frantic about it to-day, and it is impossible that prospects could be more brilliant". . . .

NEW YORK

Dolby went ahead to New York, where he found even greater enthusiasm. On the night before the tickets went on sale at Steinway Hall a line of people stretched half a mile down the street, and many brought blankets and mattresses to protect themselves against the severe cold. By morning there were over five thousand in the queue, and waiters from near-by restaurants served breakfasts along the kerb. There was already squabbling in the crowd, and pushing for places—the first signs of a trouble which was aggravated by speculators and became an incurable affliction as the tour proceeded. Dolby did his best to be fair, limiting each purchaser to four tickets, but he was outwitted by the touts [ticket scalpers] who pushed dummy buyers into the line; a two-dollar seat was fetching twenty dollars or more. At the same time he was abused in the press because, Dickens said, "he can't get four thousand people into a room that holds two thousand". The tickets for the first four New York readings were sold in a few hours and Dolby had taken in $16,000. When Dickens opened with the *Carol* and *Pickwick* he was hailed as he had been in Boston. "It is absolutely impossible that we could have made a more brilliant success than we made here last night," he wrote to [William] Wills [a friend] on 10 December. "The reception was splendid, the audience bright and perceptive. I believe that I never read so well since I began.". . .

New York had grown out of recognition. "Everything in it

looks as if the order of nature were reversed, and everything grew newer every day, instead of older," he told Wills on 10 December. And a week later he sent another triumphant report on his progress. "Everybody sleighing. Everybody coming to the readings. There were at least ten thousand sleighs in the Park last Sunday. Your illustrious chief—in a red sleigh covered with furs, and drawn by a pair of fine horses covered with bells, and tearing up 14 miles of snow an hour—made an imposing appearance.". . .

The New York readings included four appearances at the Plymouth Church in Brooklyn, where the minister was Henry Ward Beecher, the celebrated preacher and brother of [Harriet Beecher Stowe,] the author of *Uncle Tom's Cabin*. Though Dickens found himself in a "comically incongruous position", with the audience "in veritable pews", he decided it was "a wonderful place to speak in". There was the usual scramble for tickets. Because of the severe cold the waiting crowd lit an immense bonfire in a narrow street of wooden houses and nearly set them on fire. While the police dealt with the blaze, there was a general fight from "which the people farthest off in the line rushed bleeding when they saw a chance of displacing others near the door, and put their mattresses in these places, and then held on by the iron railings". . . .

THE INTERNATIONAL COPYRIGHT

Dickens reported to [Wilkie] Collins that literary pirates, who had been the cause of so many disagreeable exchanges during his first American visit, were still profiting from his work; there was no hope of an authorized production of the play [the stage version of "No Thoroughfare"] as "it is being done, in some mangled form or other, everywhere". And, as he informed [Charles] Fechter, [a friend], piracy was not confined to the latest play: "wherever I go, the theatres (with my name in big letters) instantly begin playing versions of my books". He was now more resigned to such annoying exploitation, not least because he was himself making money in America. "Well," he remarked to [his friend John] Forster, "the work is hard, the climate is hard, the life is hard, but the gain is enormous."

FURTHER PUBLIC READINGS

From New York he went on to Philadelphia, Baltimore, and Washington. All went well, he wrote to James Fields [a friend], despite the fact that "the cold remains just as it was (beastly) and where it was (in my head)." While the audiences remained "ready and bright" Dickens thought they were surprised by his simple presentation. "They seem to take it ill that I don't stagger on to the platform overpowered by the spectacle before me, and the national greatness," he wrote from Philadelphia. "They are all so accustomed to do public things with a flourish of trumpets, that the notion of my coming in to read without somebody first flying up and delivering an 'Oration' about me . . . is so very unaccountable to them, that sometimes they have no idea until I open my lips that it can possibly be Charles Dickens." In Baltimore it snowed for a day and a night, and Dickens realized that he lacked the strength to complete the original itinerary through Chicago and Canada in weather so bitterly cold. George Childs, the publisher of the Philadelphia *Public Ledger*, warned him that "the people will go into fits" if he failed to go to Chicago. "I would rather they went into fits than I did," Dickens pointedly replied, and he bore in silence the gibes of Chicago newspapers which claimed he avoided the city because his brother Augustus had left a common-law wife and three children without support when he had died in Chicago a year before. Dolby and James Osgood, who was loaned from the staff of Ticknor and Fields to assist Dickens, were "lashed into madness" by the unjustified taunts. They knew that Dickens had long supported his brother's abandoned wife, and also sent money to his Chicago dependants. "I have imposed silence upon them," Dickens wrote to Georgina [his sister-in-law] "and they really writhe under it." He valued the loyalty and companionship of his assistants all the more because he refused social invitations to conserve his energy for the readings, and Dolby and Osgood were his main resource against loneliness. . . .

All through his life Dickens was a man of resilient temper, able to work himself into a cheerful mood though he was weary and unwell. As he told Georgina in early February it was this ability to "come up to scratch" which enabled him to cope with the rigors of winter journeys and the demands of the platform. He was in Washington for his fifty-sixth birthday. "It was observed as much as though I were a little boy," he happily told Mamie [his daughter]. "Flowers and garlands . . . bloomed all over the room; letters radiant with good wishes poured in"; and there were gold and silver presents on the dinner-table. Early in the day he was received by President [Andrew] Johnson, "a man with a very remarkable and determined face", who had booked a whole row for his family at each of the Washington readings. In the afternoon, when the politician Charles Sumner called on him, Dickens was prostrate and voiceless, and Dolby was applying a mustard plaster. It seemed impossible for him to read that night. All the same, he reported to Mamie, after five minutes at the reading-desk he was not even hoarse, and "the whole audience rose and remained (Secretaries of State, President's family, Judges of the Supreme Court, and so forth) standing and cheering until I went back to the table and made them a little speech". He had come to rely upon such bursts of effective energy. "The frequent experience of this return of force when it is wanted saves me a vast amount of anxiety," he confided to Mamie, "but I am not at times without the nervous dread that I may some day sink altogether." Among other stimulants he had been fortified by "Rocky Mountain Sneezers", which he described to Fechter as "compounded of all the spirits ever heard of in the world, with bitters, lemon, sugar and snow". . . .

Dickens . . . decided to cancel the readings planned for the first week in March and to take a holiday, for February had been an exhausting month and he was due to swing out through New England to Niagara Falls and back again. There was, moreover, continuing trouble about the ticket allocations. . . . [A] clerk whom Dolby had brought out from England to assist him, was caught speculating in seats and taking bribes from would-be purchasers. Dickens himself had to run down to Providence to make an appeasing speech, and in New Haven there was a riot at the box-office and the city's mayor presided over a protest meeting. In this case Dickens refunded the money which Dolby had already taken and postponed the reading for six weeks. . . .

The nights released by the cancelled readings provided an opportunity for . . . social occasions. [Henry Wadsworth] Longfellow [the American poet] gave a dinner for him and Dickens reciprocated. "It is the established joke that Boston is 'my native place' and we hold all sorts of hearty foregatherings," he wrote to [his friend William] Macready. The weather was so foul, with gales and blizzards, that he left Boston on 6 March, a day earlier than intended, and travelled straight through to Syracuse. He described the town to [Charles] Fechter as "a most wonderful out-of-the-world place, which looks as if it had begun to be built yesterday and were going to be imperfectly knocked together with a nail or two the day after tomorrow". The hotel was bad in all respects—"quite a triumph in that way", he told Georgina— and the party sat up late playing whist and cribbage to stay out of their rooms as long as possible. "We had an old buffalo for supper," Dickens said, complaining that the menu was all the more grotesque for being written in French, "and an old pig for breakfast.". . .

DICKENS'S EXHAUSTION

Although the readings were simply produced, Dickens needed his own staff to cope with them. Apart from Dolby, who came and went about his ticket business, he was usually accompanied by Osgood, his valet and dresser Scott, George the gasman, who attended to the lighting, a couple of clerks, and a boy or two. At Niagara Falls, much impressed by his second sight of the chasm, he declared a two-day holiday for his team and sent them all sightseeing before they turned for home: "it is nearly all 'back' now, Thank God," he wrote to Forster. . . . On the days when he gave a reading he was "pretty well knocked up" [tired out] when he returned to his hotel; and the travelling conditions had deteriorated. He returned to Albany through deep floods which seriously delayed his train and marooned others. And at Albany he realized that the old trouble had broken out in his left foot and that it seemed to be spreading to the right one as well. He blamed it, as before, on walking in melted snow. It both pained and lamed him, but he went on through Boston to Portland and New Bedford. It was snowing again and his catarrh [inflammation of the throat] came back as severely as before. "I have coughed from two or three in the morning until five or six," he wrote to Mamie on 29 March, "and have been absolutely sleepless. I have had no appetite besides, and no taste. Last night here I took some laudanum [medicine with opium], and it is the only thing that has done me good." The next day he sent an equally distressed letter to Forster. "I am nearly used up," he admitted. "Climate, distance, catarrh, travelling, and hard work, have begun (I may say so, now they are nearly all over) to tell heavily upon me. Sleeplessness besets me:

and if I had engaged to go on into May I think I should have broken down."

FAREWELL TO AMERICA

Dickens knew that he was on the verge of collapse and that he had been wise to cut Canada out of his itinerary—though the compulsion to go on reading was so strong that, at the same time he was complaining to his family and friends, he was corresponding . . . about an autumn tour in England. . . . At the final reading on 8 April, before an audience packed with Boston's notability, he gave "Dr. Marigold's Prescriptions" and the "Mrs. Gamp" sketch. When the applause died away he made a brief and touching speech. "My gracious and generous welcome in America, which can never be obliterated from my remembrance, began here," he said. "My departure begins here too; for I assure you that I have never until this moment really felt that I am going away. In this brief life of ours it is sad to do almost anything for the last time, and I cannot conceal from you, although my face will so soon be turned towards my native land, and to all that makes it dear, that it is a sad consideration with me that in a few moments from this time this brilliant hall and all that it contains will fade from my view for evermore."

He was to sail from New York on 22 April, and he insisted on giving his promised readings in the city before he left. The effort and excitement so raised his blood pressure that each night he seemed likely to be struck down by apoplexy [loss of consciousness], and his right foot had become so painfully swollen that he had to lean on Dolby as he walked out to read. . . . By 18 April, when he was to be the guest of honour at a press banquet at Delmonico's, he was unable to wear his boot and his attendance seemed doubtful. Dolby drove about town looking for a gout [disease of inflamed joints] bandage, and he eventually borrowed one which Dr. Barker used to patch Dickens up for the evening. He arrived at the restaurant an hour late and entered limping on the arm of Horace Greeley, who was to preside.

It was a magnificent feast, with dishes named for famous authors and confectionery models of the Dickens characters. . . . When Dickens rose to reply to the toast he made handsome amends for the critical mood in which he had last left the United States, saying that it was henceforth his duty "to express my high and grateful sense of my second reception in America, and to bear my honest testimony to the national generosity and magnaminity". He had seen great changes. "Nor am I, I believe, so arrogant as to suppose that in twenty-five years there have been no changes in me, and that I had nothing to learn and no extreme impressions to correct when I was here first." He had been overwhelmed "with unsurpassable politeness, delicacy, sweet temper, hospitality, consideration, and with unsurpassable respect for the privacy daily enforced upon me by the nature of my avocation here and the state of my health". This glowing testimony, he promised, would be published as an appendix in each future edition of *American Notes* and *Martin Chuzzlewit.* "And this I will do and cause to be done, not in mere love and thankfulness, but because I regard it as an act of plain justice and honour." There remained only a peroration [speech] on the common heritage: "better for this globe to be riven by an earthquake, fired by a comet, overrun by an iceberg, and abandoned to the Arctic fox and bear, than that it should present the spectacle of these two great nations, each of which has, in its own way and hour, striven so hard and so successfully for freedom, ever again being arrayed one against the other."

When Dickens finished and the applause died away he excused himself, for he was in too much pain to stay for the remaining speeches. He had still to make his last appearance on 20 April, and before an audience of over two thousand people he ended his tour as he had begun it, with the *Carol* and *Pickwick.* "I beg to bid you farewell," he said when he was finished, "and I pray God bless you, and God bless the land in which I leave you."

Two days later, on a sparkling spring day, Dickens went through the crowd which waited outside the Westminster Hotel to the private tug which took him to the *Russia,* moored out by Staten Island. . . .

It was a rough passage home, but the rest and sea air were a much needed tonic. Within four days Dickens was free of his catarrh and able to put a shoe on his right foot; and when he arrived in Liverpool he looked bronzed and fit. "My doctor was quite broken down in spirits when he saw me," he wrote to Mrs. [James] Fields. "'Good Lord,' he said, recoiling, 'seven years younger!'" The pile of dollars amounted to a small fortune. The seventy-six readings had grossed $228,000, or an average of $3,000 a night. After the deduction of $39,000 for expenses, and the conversion of the dollars into gold, Dickens told Forster, his profit "was within a hundred or so of £20,000". He exultantly reminded Forster that from his first readings in England he had made £10,000 and another £13,000 from those organized by Chappell's [an agency]. "These figures are of course between ourselves," he wrote, "but don't you think them rather remarkable?"

CHAPTER 5

DICKENS'S LITERARY REPUTATION

CHARLES DICKENS

Homage to Dickens

Robert B. Partlow Jr.

Written by Robert B. Partlow Jr., this survey of responses to Dickens's death in 1870 emphasizes the grief and bereavement expressed by the millions of nineteenth-century worldwide readers of Dickens, who regarded him as their favorite writer. His loss was felt by them to mark the end of an epoch. Yet Dickens was buried without any pomp. He disclaimed monuments, wanting to be commemorated only by his writings.

Many of Dickens's contemporaries thought that the enduring worth of his literary achievements could only be assessed properly after his death. However, the process of evaluation had actually begun decades earlier, from the date of publication of his first works. Many of the obituary notices were even written by the same men of letters who had reviewed—and generally acclaimed—Dickens's novels when they appeared in print.

Robert B. Partlow Jr., associate professor of English at Southern Illinois University, has authored works on cultural studies and has edited a collection of critical essays on Dickens, in which this foreword appears.

The immediate response of English journalists and reviewers to the sudden, unexpected death of Charles Dickens in 1870 was shock and a sense of bereavement, perhaps best summed up, appropriately, in the *Times* for 10 June:

> One whom young and old, wherever the English language is spoken, have been accustomed to regard as a personal friend is suddenly taken away from us. CHARLES DICKENS is no more. The loss of such a man makes ordinary expressions of regret seem cold and conventional. It will be felt by millions as nothing less than a personal bereavement. Statesmen, men of science, philanthropists, the acknowledged benefactors of their

Robert B. Partlow Jr., "Foreword," *Dickens the Craftsman: Strategies of Presentation*, edited by Robert B. Partlow Jr. Carbondale: Southern Illinois University Press, 1970. Copyright © 1970 by Southern Illinois University Press. Reproduced by permission.

race might pass away, and yet not leave the void which will be caused by the death of DICKENS. They may have earned the esteem of mankind; their days may have been passed in power, honour, and prosperity; they may have been surrounded by troops of friends, but however preeminent in station, ability, or public services, they will not have been, like our great and genial novelist, the intimate of every household.

Other newspapers and magazines wrote of the loss not only as of a personal friend, but as of the end of something deeply significant, even if not fully understood. The leader in the *Illustrated London News* for 18 June began:

> The death . . . of a great author whose books have given pleasure to more readers in his lifetime than those of any other English writer, is an event that stirs up mixed feelings in the mind. There is a sense of sudden loss. . . . There is an intimate and heartfelt consciousness of personal loss in the recollection of our past frequent communion with a favourite author, who has come to us a hundred times, bringing always new thoughts or new shapes of fancy, new expressions of feeling. He will never again offer anything new for our entertainment, though we may turn back to him as often as we please to let him repeat what he has offered us before.

Among many other personal responses, Anthony Trollope's is remarkable since he was not only a novelist himself but a close friend of Dickens, only four years younger than the [William Makepeace] Thackeray whose obituary he sorrowfully wrote in 1863 and three years younger than Dickens, whose obituary he sadly offered up in *St. Paul's*. His last paragraph reads:

> A great man has gone from us;—such a one that we may surely say of him that we shall not look on his like again. As years roll on, we shall learn to appreciate his loss. He now rests in the spot consecrated to the memory of our greatest and noblest; and English men would certainly not have been contented had he been laid elsewhere.

DICKENS: A FRIEND BELOVED BY ALL

Most of the editorials, obituaries, and articles written within a few weeks of Dickens' death speak of him in much the same way: a great man, a great writer, a friend to every Englishman of every class, a man who contributed greatly to his country, has died, and the nation is the less for that death. Many of the published pieces memorialize him by reviewing the more public characteristics of the man, by perpetuating (sometimes by creating) a public biography. Sir Arthur Helps' comments are typical of this approach; his initial sentence is, "When a great man departs from us, what we desire to know about him is not so much what he did, as what he was." Like others, he mentions Dickens' powers of observation, his imaginative powers, his punctilious accuracy, his love of order and neatness, his toleration and kindness exhibited in real life as well as in his writings, his lively interest in important public affairs, his habit of telling the truth even to himself, his love of the poor and oppressed, and his talents as an actor and public speaker. [In an obituary written in July 1870,] Sir Arthur insists that

> I have done my best to describe Mr. Dickens as he appeared to me, and certainly I have not uttered one word of flattery. But who can describe a great man—or indeed any man? We map down his separate qualities; but the subtle combination of them made by Nature eludes our description; and, after all, we fail, as I have failed now, in bringing before the reader the full sweetness, lovingness, and tenderness, wit and worth and sagacity, of such man as Charles Dickens, whose death is not merely a private grief—unspeakable, irreparable—to his family and many friends, but a public sorrow which all nations unite in deploring.

John Forster's massive biography of his longtime friend and colleague is, of course, the major product of this sort of response to Dickens, and [is] supplemented by the memorials, letters, reminiscences of other friends and colleagues. . . . In this respect all of them were carrying out the instructions left by Dickens in his will, quoted in part by Dean [Arthur] Stanley during his memorial sermon in Westminster Abbey:

> I direct that my name be inscribed in plain English letters on my tomb. . . . I enjoin my friends on no account to make me the subject of any monument, memorial, or testimonial whatever. I rest my claims to the remembrance of my country upon my published works, and the remembrance of my friends upon their experience of me in addition thereto.

In all probability Dickens was alluding in his will to monuments like that of Sir Walter Scott, that pile of stone rivaled only by the Albert Memorial—and this wish was respected. But there are other forms of monumentalization almost inevitable after the death of a great man, especially if he was greatly loved or greatly admired. There seems to be some ingrained need to *fix* the man and his work, to abstract him as the sculptor does, to smooth out the rough spots, to establish a final pose and posture, to create a satisfying image of the

ASSESSING DICKENS

Critical evaluation of Dickens's novels may prove to be a difficult task since they neither fit easily into widely accepted categories of classification nor conform to conventional aesthetic norms. Some critics consider Dickens's novels to be insufficiently serious and overly sentimental. Yet perhaps our contemporary criteria of judgment should be scrutinized, and even modified, in order to more fairly assess Dickens's achievements. This is the argument advanced by Martin Price, who was professor of English at Yale University. He wrote numerous studies of eighteenth- and nineteenth-century British writers and edited the volume of critical essays on Dickens from which this introduction is taken.

There is no term that recurs more often in recent Dickens criticism than "Shakespearean," for the comparison is an almost inevitable way of defining some of Dickens' powers: his effortless invention, his brilliant play of language, the scope and density of his imagined world. The comparison serves to identify those powers all would grant; and it helps also to free Dickens' work from false expectations—that he is, or should be, writing the kind of novel George Eliot or Henry James wrote. Throughout English criticism, the example of Shakespeare confounds critical dogmatism. It makes us ask ourselves what we have achieved when we have created a critical system that disables us for reading our greatest writers.

So it is in the case of Dickens. As the nineteenth century novel began to seek the dignity of high art, the pleasures of Dickens did not seem adequately "serious," and his novels became the experience of the nursery. Those who later rejected Victorian sentiment and morality were disdainful of the creator of the Christmas books or the death of Little Nell and overlooked, as best they could, the vehement satirist of Podsnappery and the Circumlocution Office. As best they could: there were always some to take him seriously. [Playwright George] Bernard Shaw considered *Little Dorrit* "a more seditious book than *Das Kapital*" [by Karl Marx]. What we are coming belatedly to see is that *Little Dorrit* is seditious in more than a political sense. It requires us to examine most of our conceptions of what the novel should be, and, as we turn back to Dickens from [Fyodor] Dostoevsky or [Franz] Kafka, from [playwright Bertolt] Brecht or the theater of the absurd, we are better able to see some of what has been there all the time.

Martin Price, ed., introduction to *Dickens: A Collection of Critical Essays.* Englewood Cliffs, NJ: Prentice-Hall, 1967, p. 1.

man for his age and for the future. The real, mercurial, contradictory man was gone, interred and honored as a national figure; the memory of the man was lovingly recalled, explained, embellished, and gradually fixed; books, letters, manuscripts, remains, were deposited in the national archives as relics. There remained the task of estimating his lasting worth—and that began as soon as he was dead, indeed had begun among the journalists as early as the first reviews of *Pickwick Papers;* now the corpus of work was complete, and assessments could be made without fear of contradiction by the next series of numbers. . . .

EARLY ASSESSMENTS OF HIS WORK

What is most striking to the student who investigates the early essays on Dickens' work is the prevalence of *literary* criticism (or, more strictly, critical response) which is remarkably similar to work being done in our time, though clearly less complete, less rigorous in method, and less penetrating. . . . Dickens has been considered a craftsman, an artist, even a poet, almost from the beginning of his career. As early as 1851 some reviewers and critics were discussing Dickens in terms of the art of the novel and not merely as a humorist, a reformer, or an entertainer; and by the 1860's and seventies many of the avenues now being assiduously explored were identified, though only sketchily mapped.

The reviewers who wrote the obituary notices in 1870 surely did not arrive at their conclusions about Dickens on the spur of the moment; what they said quite probably comprised the general conclusions of their group over the preceding twenty or thirty years. When they sat down to make their final pronouncements, they did not have to search for things to say about their long-familiar friend and mentor. As one editor [of the *Illustrated London News*] said,

> His method of composing and publishing his tales in monthly parts, or sometimes in weekly parts, aided the experience of this immediate personal companionship between the writer and the reader. It was just as if we received a letter or a visit, at regular intervals, from a kindly, observant gossip . . . who would let us know from time to time what was going on. . . . This periodical and piecemeal form of publication, being attended by a fragmentary manner of composition, was not at all favourable to the artistic harmony of his work as a whole. But few persons ever read any of Dickens's stories as a whole for the first time; because everyone was eager to enjoy the

parts as they were printed, going on a twelve month or twenty months in due succession, and growing in popularity as the pile of them increased.

Despite the demurrer about the organic unity of Dickens' novels, apparently a fairly common response during his lifetime and only recently disposed of, this reviewer insists that "he was not merely a writer of extraordinary talent and skill; but, he was also a man of genius—let us say a prose poet.". . .

To be accurate, the most common terms applied to Dickens and his work are "humorist" and "moralist," rather typically expressed in the *Spectator* [of 1870]:

> The greatest humourist whom England ever produced,—Shakespeare himself not excepted,—is gone. . . . Humour,—in his case certainly, and we believe it has almost always been so,—is a great solvent of all exclusiveness and intolerance, a great enemy to social, to moral, to religious bigotry. . . . He has taught us by his humour, as nothing else could have taught us, how full to overflowing what is called "vulgar" life is of all the human qualities, good and evil, which make up the interest of human existence.

But a surprising amount of space in the journals is devoted to the literary aspects of Dickens' work, even to technical and stylistic elements. In fact, as I suggested earlier, many of the areas now being scrutinized were adumbrated at this time. The starting point seems to have been the realization that Dickens handled words in a fresh, exciting manner, like an artist, a prose poet, manipulating language to achieve the pictorial and emotional effects he desired. To be exact, most of the critics' emphasis was on the characters and the "political" content, that is, on the meanings expressed by those words, which is only to be expected in critical estimates of a novelist who is advocating "radical" solutions for current problems.

The Genius of Dickens

Barbara Hardy

Barbara Hardy, a well-known scholar and professor
of English at London University, has published various studies of nineteenth-century British novelists,
including two books on Dickens. She maintains that
Dickens has many of the characteristics attributed to
Shakespeare. Dickens has influenced twentieth-
century writers, and his novels, so theatrical in nature, have frequently been adapted for film, stage,
and television.

Hardy points out that Dickens's focus in his novels
is simultaneously inward and outward: He experi-
mented with the psychological portrayal of characters, attempting to reveal both their inner lives and
their outer appearance, garb, and gestures. At the
same time, few writers have succeeded to the degree
that Dickens has in depicting Victorian society and
exposing its corruption.

One of the greatest modern writers, James Joyce, claimed
that Dickens has entered into the language more than any
writer since Shakespeare. This is not mere praise. Like
Shakespeare, Dickens brims with originality, but expresses
and addresses human nature at large. Like Shakespeare, he
is fully in possession of himself, creating an art that is powerfully personal and generously accessible. Like Shakespeare, he creates a flexible language for self-expression
and imaginative creativity that commands admiration for its
brilliance and virtuosity. Like Shakespeare, he creates a
unique and independent-seeming world, allowing us to use
that time-worn term "world" with precision.

HISTORIAN OF VICTORIAN SOCIETY

Dickens has entered into the art and consciousness of modern writers such as Joyce, T.S. Eliot, Evelyn Waugh, George

Barbara Hardy, *Charles Dickens: The Writer and His Work.* Windsor: Profile Books,
1983. Copyright © 1983 by Barbara Hardy. Reproduced by permission.

Orwell, and Angus Wilson, but has also been assimilated without too much damage into popular culture and media such as film, radio, and television. His myths are old and new, Victorian and modern. Pickwick, Mrs. Gamp, Quilp, and Oliver Twist are only a few of his many popular fictions, individual and typical, comic and terrible. Such characters can stand as models or reminders of his own genius, for, like their author, they combined peculiarity with ordinariness. Their ancestors are Falstaff, Lady Macbeth, Iago, and Hamlet; like them, they speak with the force and simplicity of moral abstractions but are imagined as individuals with appropriate voice and form. They carry history with them: it is hard to think of the wretched Victorian orphan or the workhouse without remembering Oliver and his porridge bowl, of the Victorian capitalist without remembering Dombey and his son, of sly or brutal crime without remembering Fagin and Bill Sikes, of prison without remembering the Dorrits, of the newly rich without remembering the Veneerings, of cant and prudishness without Podsnap. Their very names are vivid metonymies [a literary term in which one word stands for another word that it suggests, so that "Fagin" becomes a term for a criminal, "Podsnap" for a prude]. For many readers, Dickens is not only a great novelist but a history book. Victorian England is his "best of times" and "worst of times," though the sentence in which he used those words at the beginning of *A Tale of Two Cities* (1859) was not referring to his epoch or his society. His fictions are packed with social information and social passion. . . .

PORTRAYING THE PSYCHOLOGY OF CHARACTERS

Robert Garis, in *The Dickens Theatre*, has discussed that frank and open theatricality with which Dickens presents and animates his work. Theatricality is a useful word to describe the vitality and flourish of his appearances as an author, and useful too in defining the limits of his art. We should insist on these limits not because Dickens has been over-praised, but in order to try to recognize his individuality. He is theatrical, for instance, in his use of external action. His stage is not often the lonely stage of soliloquy, but a stage crowded with the lively, stereotyped, stagey, concrete, simplified, physically exciting actions of actors. Dickens provides not only script and stage directions but movement and performances too. His novels are like plays in action. But in the novels from *Dombey and Son* onward, he seems to be pushing this theatrical and extrovert art beyond the limits of theatricality. The attempt to imply the inner life of characters can be traced back to Sikes and Ralph Nickleby, but becomes fully developed in Dombey and Edith, who are shown stagily but subtly. It continues in the figure of Esther Summerson whom Dickens is trying to create from the inside, though often with the unhappy result of making a reserved and introspective character behave like a self-conscious puppet. *Bleak House* is a valiant failure in an attempt to show the inner life of a human being in one part of the novel, and an impersonal, fierce vision of social injustice in the other. In *Hard Times* he places his analysis of the inner life most courageously and effectively in a simple fable and shows it, as in *Dombey and Son*, not through the technique of enlarged soliloquy, where he is generally weak, but through implication and reticence, where he is strong.

The psychology becomes more complex and mobile in content as he goes on experimenting in form: in *Little Dorrit* we have the inner self of Clennam's vivid ordinariness, and Dickens moves from this success to others, in Pip and Wrayburn. He is exploring a kind of character really belonging to another kind of novel, very far from theatrical, that novel of inner action written by Charlotte Brontë, George Eliot, George Meredith, and Henry James, where the very form of the novel takes on the imprint of consciousness. Dickens' persistent experiments are marked by a limitation. He is apparently not trying to write whole novels of inner action, but inserting this inner analysis of complexity into *his* kind of novel, placing its subtlety under the spotlight that glares on the Dickens stage. Sometimes he can only bring it off for short stretches, as with the childhood of David; sometimes he manages the marvellous sleight-of-hand that makes us feel we have had full access to the conflicts of Dombey, Edith and Louisa. Sometimes he creates the dense particularity of Pip, Clennam, Wrayburn. But it is a dense particularity revealed by his own weird spotlight. And it keeps strange company, which is not complex or dense, or always very individualized. It is the story of an inner life, rather than the presentation of an inner life.

It points to three things: first, to that theatrical and extrovert nature of his genius. Next, it reveals his delight in difficulty, in the strenuousness spoken of by Henry James that

shows itself so energetically in Dickens' attempt to push beyond the frontiers of his genius. Finally, it is no accident that
in those novels where he succeeds in actualizing a central
character, we feel least troubled by the duality and disparity
of his analysis of the individual and the society. His develop-
ing interest in psychology seems at times to go against the
grain of his genius, but in fact his sociological imagination
needed the particulars of a sense of character and is badly
betrayed and isolated when Dickens fails to anatomize the
single heart. It is that powerful sociological imagination that
triumphs most truthfully when Dickens succeeds in pierc-
ing through to the inner life. Dickens the man was often
muddled, inconsistent, and neurotic in his responses to political problems and social experience, but at its best his art
overcame or sublimated the weaknesses of the artist.

DISCUSSION QUESTIONS

CHAPTER 1

1. Discuss the significance of the two events, described by Edgar Johnson, that occurred when Dickens was twelve. Why was the experience of the blacking factory so traumatic for young Dickens? Why was his misery intensified by what happened to his father? Show what the two events have in common.

2. Compare or contrast the conclusions of Edgar Johnson and Peter Ackroyd regarding the impact of Dickens's childhood on his adult life. According to the two scholars, was this impact only negative, or did it have any positive benefits? Would Dickens have been a better writer had he experienced a happy childhood? Give reasons for your conclusions.

3. Frank Donovan and Peter Ackroyd both suggest that Dickens's childhood vision of the world shaped his fiction in various specific ways. How did it do so? What evidence does each scholar provide for this conclusion? Do you find this evidence persuasive? Explain why or why not.

CHAPTER 2

1. According to Angus Wilson, why did Dickens criticize Parliament? Why did he oppose revolution? How can these two views be reconciled? Explain why Dickens's opinions were considered conservative rather than radical.

2. Referring to Philip Collins's article, explain what is meant by the term "workhouse school." Why did Dickens criticize Victorian workhouse schools? What qualities would he expect to find in an ideal workhouse school?

3. Why did Graham Storey argue that *Bleak House* should be considered in its proper historical context? What topical issues are discussed in the novel? Specify. How are the issues relevant to the novel's literary merit?

4. What were the various paths to social reform open to Dickens, as set forth by Ivor Brown? Which one did Dickens choose, and why? What did Dickens demand of his fellow Englishmen in his campaign for social reform? Why does Brown consider Dickens an optimistic reformer? How does this assertion differ from that of Flint?

5. With reference to Louis Cazamian's article, what specific social evils did Dickens criticize in his novels? What role did Dickens's readers play in his campaign against specific abuses? What effect did Dickens's writing have on British law? Give details.

6. Cite evidence from the article by Kate Flint to show how Dickens's views of human nature were contradictory. How did these views affect his belief in the amelioration of society?

CHAPTER 3

1. In Ivor Brown's view, what was the crucial factor in Dickens's novels that differentiated him from his predecessors? How did the concerns of Dickens's novels differ from those of Jane Austen and Sir Walter Scott? In what way did Dickens's concerns resemble those of Henrik Ibsen?

2. Referring to Michael Wheeler's description of the conditions under which books were published during the Victorian era, explain why such vast numbers of novels were published each year. Show how the cost of reading was reduced in England from the early to mid–nineteenth century.

3. According to John Butt and Kathleen Tillotson, what work methods did Dickens adopt to cope with the stringent requirements of serial publication? What were the advantages and disadvantages of serial publication for the writer? What were the benefits for the reader?

4. Fred Kaplan argues that in *David Copperfield* Dickens created a fictionalized version of his own life. Show precisely how he did so, citing specific evidence from Kaplan's article. Kaplan also contends that by writing in middle age about the traumatic wounds of his childhood and young adulthood, Dickens was able to exorcise them. Explain why you agree or disagree with this conclusion.

5. In his discussion of Dickens's major works of the 1850s, Allan Grant writes, "In these novels, social misery is no longer laid at the door of evil individuals, but is felt to be part of the fabric of a rotten society." Analyze what is meant by Grant's comment and give examples from his

article to support your points. How did the British government's treatment of its own soldiers during the Crimean War exemplify the "rotten society" criticized by Dickens in his novels?

6. Citing evidence from Edmund Wilson's article, explain how Dickens imaginatively enacted the roles of both criminal and rebel. Why did Dickens link these two figures in his mind? Show how Dickens's opinions on prisons, prisoners, and punishment revealed his attitude toward the criminal. Discuss the extent to which Dickens's political views exemplified his attitude toward the rebel.

CHAPTER 4

1. According to Michael Slater, how did Dickens define the proper role of women? Why did he consider any campaign for women's rights unnatural? Discuss the reasons why modern feminists might find Dickens's attitude offensive.

2. Martin Fido asserts that Dickens was a "laureate of home and hearth" to his readers. Explain what is meant by this phrase, and show how Dickens's behavior throughout 1857 and 1858 served to subvert the values conveyed by his novels. Give details of the breakdown of his marriage, where relevant, to support your argument. Assess both Catherine Dickens and Ellen Ternan, as described by Fido, in terms of Dickens's conception of the Victorian womanly ideal, as discussed by Slater.

3. Emlyn Williams contends that Dickens's genius was actually directed to the theater and dramatic expression. Why, then, did Dickens not write plays instead of novels? Explain how Dickens was thwarted by the character of the age in which he lived. In what ways did Dickens succeed in involving himself in the theater after he became a successful novelist?

4. Show how Williams's discussion of Dickens's genius is relevant to his reading tour of the United States, as described by Norman and Jean MacKenzie. What did Dickens accomplish on this reading tour?

CHAPTER 5

1. Robert B. Partlow Jr. discusses the assessment of Dickens as a writer by his contemporaries. Which of Dickens's qualities and literary achievements were praised most highly by Victorian men of letters? Would a modern critic

reviewing Dickens's work today appraise Dickens in the same way? Give evidence to support your opinion.

2. Explain Barbara Hardy's distinction between the outward "theatricality" of Dickens's fictional characters and their "inner life." Why does Hardy argue that Dickens's increasing interest in psychology was incompatible with the sociological emphasis of his novels? Show why you do or do not agree. What similarities does Hardy find between Dickens and William Shakespeare?

APPENDIX OF DOCUMENTS

DOCUMENT 1: DAVID COPPERFIELD IS SENT OUT TO WORK

In this excerpt from David Copperfield, *the most autobiographical of Dickens's novels, the first-person narrator's moving account of being sent out to work in a warehouse is easily recognizable as a fictionalized version of Dickens's own boyhood experience in a blacking factory. Moreover, as young Copperfield describes his misery and humiliation, his words not only echo but repeat, almost word-for-word, Dickens's account of his own youthful suffering (an account found in the famous autobiographical manuscript sent to his friend and biographer John Forster).*

I KNOW enough of the world now, to have almost lost the capacity of being much surprised by anything; but it is [a] matter of some surprise to me, even now, that I can have been so easily thrown away at such an age. A child of excellent abilities, and with strong powers of observation, quick, eager, delicate, and soon hurt bodily or mentally, it seems wonderful to me that nobody should have made any sign in my behalf. But none was made; and I became, at ten years old, a little labouring hind in the service of Murdstone and Grinby.

Murdstone and Grinby's warehouse was at the waterside. It was down in Blackfriars. Modern improvements have altered the place; but it was the last house at the bottom of a narrow street, curving down hill to the river, with some stairs at the end, where people took boat. It was a crazy old house with a wharf of its own, abutting on the water when the tide was in, and on the mud when the tide was out, and literally overrun with rats. Its panelled rooms, discoloured with the dirt and smoke of a hundred years, I dare say; its decaying floors and staircase; the squeaking and scuffling of the old grey rats down in the cellars; and the dirt and rottenness of the place; are things, not of many years ago, in my mind, but of the present instant. They are all before me, just as they were in the evil hour when I went among them for the first time, with my trembling hand in Mr Quinion's [his supervisor].

Murdstone and Grinby's trade was among a good many kinds of people, but an important branch of it was the supply of wines and spirits to certain packet ships. I forget now where they chiefly went, but I think there were some among them that made voyages both to the East and West Indies. I know that a great many empty bottles

189

were one of the consequences of this traffic, and that certain men and boys were employed to examine them against the light, and reject those that were flawed, and to rinse and wash them. When the empty bottles ran short, there were labels to be pasted on full ones, or corks to be fired to them, or seals to be put upon the corks, or finished bottles to be packed in casks. All this work was my work, and of the boys employed upon it I was one.

There were three or four of us, counting me. My working place was established in a corner of the warehouse, where Mr Quinion could see me, when he chose to stand up on the bottom rail of his stool in the counting-house, and look at me through a window above the desk. Hither, on the first morning of my so auspiciously beginning life on my own account, the oldest of the regular boys was summoned to show me my business. His name was Mick Walker, and he wore a ragged apron and a paper cap. He informed me that his father was a bargeman. . . . He also informed me that our principal associate would be another boy whom he introduced by the—to me—extraordinary name of Mealy Potatoes. I discovered, however, that this youth had not been christened by that name, but that it had been bestowed upon him in the warehouse, on account of his complexion, which was pale or mealy. Mealy's father was a waterman. . . .

No words can express the secret agony of my soul as I sunk into this companionship; compared these henceforth everyday associates with those of my happier childhood . . . and felt my hopes of growing up to be a learned and distinguished man, crushed in my bosom. The deep remembrance of the sense I had, of being utterly without hope now; of the shame I felt in my position; of the misery it was to my young heart to believe that day by day what I had learned, and thought, and delighted in, and raised my fancy and my emulation up by, would pass away from me, little by little, never to be brought back any more; cannot be written. As often as Mick Walker went away in the course of that forenoon, I mingled my tears with the water in which I was washing the bottles; and sobbed as if there were a flaw in my own breast, and it were in danger of bursting.

Charles Dickens, *The Personal History of David Copperfield*, ed. Trevor Blount. New York: Penguin, 1966.

DOCUMENT 2: SPURNED BY HIS FIRST LOVE

In 1830, at the age of eighteen, Dickens first met Maria Beadnell, an attractive, flirtatious young woman of twenty, the youngest daughter of a prosperous family. As a welcome guest at the Beadnells' home, Dickens misjudged the extent of their social acceptance. When he fell in love with Maria, it became evident that her parents did not regard him as an eligible suitor: He was the son of a bankrupt, and his own financial prospects in 1832 as a parliamentary reporter were not promising. Maria was sent abroad in 1832, and when she returned home in 1833 she no longer took Dickens's courtship seriously. Dickens reveals his bitter disappointment, resentment, and wounded pride in these highly emotional passages, taken from two of his letters to Maria Beadnell, in which he reproaches her for her fickle behavior, even as he continues to passionately proclaim his love for her, but to no avail. Maria's rejection long remained a painful memory to Dickens, undermining his self-confidence and self-esteem.

March 18th 1833

DEAR MISS BEADNELL,—Your own feelings will enable you to imagine far better than any attempt of mine to describe the painful struggle it has cost me to make up my mind to adopt the course which I now take—a course than which nothing can be so directly opposed to my wishes and feelings, but the necessity of which becomes daily more apparent to me. Our meetings of late have been little more than so many displays of heartless indifference on the one hand, while on the other they have never failed to prove a fertile source of wretchedness and misery; and seeing, as I cannot fail to do, that I have engaged in a pursuit which has long since been worse than hopeless and a further perseverance in which can only expose me to deserved ridicule, I have made up my mind to return the little present I received from you some time since (which I have always prized, as I still do, far beyond anything I ever possessed) and the other enclosed mementos of our past correspondence which I am sure it must be gratifying to you to receive, as after our recent situations they are certainly better adapted for your custody than mine.

Need I say that I have not the most remote idea of hurting your feelings by the few lines which I think it necessary to write with the accompanying little parcel? I must be the last person in the world who could entertain such an intention, but I feel that this is neither a matter nor a time for cold, deliberate, calculating trifling. *My* feelings upon any subject more especially upon this, must be to you a matter of very little moment; still *I have* feelings in common with other people—perhaps so far as they relate to you they have been as strong and as good as ever warmed the human heart—and I do feel that it is mean and contemptible of me to keep by me one gift of yours or to preserve one single line or word of remembrance, or affection from you. I therefore return them, and I can only wish that I could as easily forget that I ever received them. . . .

19th May 1833

DEAR MISS BEADNELL,—I am anxious to take the earliest opportunity of writing you again. . . . I have considered and reconsidered the matter, and I have come to the unqualified determination that I will allow no feeling of pride, no haughty dislike to making a conciliation to prevent my expressing it without reserve. I will advert to nothing that has passed, I will not again seek to excuse any part

I have acted or to justify it by any course you have ever pursued; I will revert to nothing that has ever passed between us—I will only openly and at once say that there is nothing I have more at heart, nothing I more sincerely and earnestly desire, than to be reconciled to you. It would be useless for me to repeat here what I have so often said before; it would be equally useless to look forward and state my hopes for the future—all that anyone can do to raise himself by his own exertions and unceasing assiduity I have done, and will do. I have no guide by which to ascertain your present feelings and I have, God knows, no means of influencing them in my favour. I never have loved and I can never love any human creature breathing but yourself. We have had many differences, and we have lately been entirely separated. Absence, however, has not altered my feelings in the slightest degree, and the Love I now tender you is as pure and as lasting as at any period of our former correspondence. I have now done all I can to remove our most unfortunate and to me most unhappy misunderstanding. The matter now of course rests solely with you, and you will decide as your own feelings and wishes direct you. I could say much for myself and I could entreat a favourable consideration on my own behalf but I purposely abstain from doing so because it would be only a repetition of an oft told tale and because I am sure that nothing I could say would have the effect of influencing your decision in any degree whatever. Need I say that to me it is a matter of vital import and the most intense anxiety?—I fear that the numerous claims which must necessarily be made on your time and attention next week will prevent your answering this note within anything like the time which my impatience would name.

Charles Dickens, *The Letters of Charles Dickens, 1832–1846*, vol. 1, ed. Walter Dexter. Bloomsbury, UK: The Nonesuch Press, 1938.

DOCUMENT 3: INSIDE A CLASSROOM

Dickens's novel Hard Times *begins here, with Sir Thomas Grad-grind, a retired hardware merchant, advocating a practical, useful, mechanistic view of education—one that is based on teaching only "facts" and, by necessitating memorizing by rote, allows for neither creativity nor individualism. Dickens's harsh criticism of this kind of pedagogic process is conveyed by his satiric treatment of Gradgrind and his views in the course of the novel. Even in this excerpt, Grad-grind is held up to ridicule as the author draws the reader's attention to his pompous, overbearing manner, as conveyed by his pointing finger, his "dictatorial" voice, and his "obstinate" stance.*

"Now, what I want is, Facts. Teach these boys and girls nothing but Facts. Facts alone are wanted in life. Plant nothing else, and root out everything else. You can only form the minds of reasoning animals upon Facts: nothing else will ever be of any service to them. This is the principle on which I bring up my own children, and this is the principle on which I bring up these children. Stick to Facts, Sir!"

The scene was a plain, bare, monotonous vault of a schoolroom, and the speaker's square forefinger emphasized his observations by underscoring every sentence with a line on the schoolmaster's sleeve. The emphasis was helped by the speaker's square wall of a forehead, which had his eyebrows for its base, while his eyes found commodious cellarage in two dark caves, overshadowed by the wall. The emphasis was helped by the speaker's mouth, which was wide, thin, and hard set. The emphasis was helped by the speaker's voice, which was inflexible, dry, and dictatorial. The emphasis was helped by the speaker's hair, which bristled on the skirts of his bald head, a plantation of firs to keep the wind from its shining surface, all covered with knobs, like the crust of a plum pie, as if the head had scarcely warehouse-room for the hard facts stored inside. The speaker's obstinate carriage, square coat, square legs, square shoulders,—nay, his very neckcloth, trained to take him by the throat with an unaccommodating grasp, like a stubborn fact, as it was,—all helped the emphasis.

"In this life, we want nothing but Facts, Sir; nothing but Facts!"

The speaker and the schoolmaster . . . backed a little, and swept with their eyes the inclined plane of little vessels [the pupils] then and there arranged in order, ready to have imperial gallons of facts poured into them until they were full to the brim.

Thomas Gradgrind, Sir. A man of realities. A man of facts and calculations. A man who proceeds upon the principle that two and two are four, and nothing over, and who is not to be talked into allowing for anything over. Thomas Gradgrind, Sir—peremptorily Thomas—Thomas Gradgrind. With a rule and a pair of scales, and the multiplication table always in his pocket, Sir, ready to weigh and measure any parcel of human nature, and tell you exactly what it comes to. It is a mere question of figures, a case of simple arithmetic. . . .

Charles Dickens, *Hard Times*. New York: E.P. Dutton, 1907.

DOCUMENT 4: A WORKHOUSE ORPHAN ASKS FOR MORE FOOD

In Oliver Twist, *Dickens severely condemns Victorian society's failure to provide adequately for its poor. One of the ways that he does so effectively in the first part of the novel is to graphically describe a workhouse, a place of refuge for paupers and orphans, where Oliver Twist and the other orphaned boys are fed a thin gruel, which leaves them undernourished and constantly hungry. In the following memorable scene, the most famous one in the novel, Oliver Twist dares to ask for more food, with dire consequences. Dickens's readers were undoubtedly aware that, although the book was a work of fiction, the deplorable conditions of the workhouse shown here provided an accurate, true-to-life picture of these institutions.*

The room in which the boys were fed, was a large stone hall, with a copper at one end: out of which the master, dressed in an apron for the purpose, and assisted by one or two women, ladled the gruel at meal-times. Of this festive composition each boy had one porringer, and no more—except on occasions of great public rejoicing, when he had two ounces and a quarter of bread besides. The bowls never wanted washing. The boys polished them with their spoons till they shone again; and when they had performed this operation (which never took very long, the spoons being nearly as large as the bowls), they would sit staring at the copper, with such eager eyes, as if they could have devoured the very bricks of which it was composed; employing themselves, meanwhile, in sucking their fingers most assiduously, with the view of catching up any stray splashes of gruel that might have been cast thereon. Boys have generally excellent appetites. Oliver Twist and his companions suffered the tortures of slow starvation for three months: at last they got so voracious and wild with hunger, that one boy, who was tall for his age, and hadn't been used to that sort of thing (for his father had kept a small cookshop), hinted darkly to his companions, that unless he had another basin of gruel *per diem* [each day], he was afraid he might some night happen to eat the boy who slept next him, who happened to be a weakly youth of tender age. He had a wild, hungry eye; and they implicitly believed him. A council was held; lots were cast who should walk up to the master after supper that evening, and ask for more; and it fell to Oliver Twist.

The evening arrived; the boys took their places. The master, in his cook's uniform, stationed himself at the copper; his pauper assistants ranged themselves behind him; the gruel was served out; and a long grace was said over the short commons. The gruel disappeared; the boys whispered each other, and winked at Oliver; while his next neighbours nudged him. Child as he was, he was desperate with hunger, and reckless with misery. He rose from the table; and advancing to the master, basin and spoon in hand, said: somewhat alarmed at his own temerity:

"Please, sir, I want some more."

The master was a fat, healthy man; but he turned very pale. He gazed in stupefied astonishment on the small rebel for some seconds, and then clung for support to the copper. The assistants were paralysed with wonder; the boys with fear.

"What!" said the master at length, in a faint voice.

"Please, sir," replied Oliver, "I want some more."

The master aimed a blow at Oliver's head with the ladle; pinioned him in his arms; and shrieked aloud for the beadle.

The board were sitting in solemn conclave, when Mr. Bumble [the master] rushed into the room in great excitement, and addressing the gentleman in the high chair, said,

"Mr. Limbkins, I beg your pardon, sir! Oliver Twist has asked for more!"

There was a general start. Horror was depicted on every countenance.

"For *more!*" said Mr. Limbkins. "Compose yourself, Bumble, and answer me distinctly. Do I understand that he asked for more, after he had eaten the supper allotted by the dietary?"

"He did, sir," replied Bumble.

"That boy will be hung," said the gentleman in the white waistcoat. "I know that boy will be hung."

Nobody controverted the prophetic gentleman's opinion. An animated discussion took place. Oliver was ordered into instant confinement; and a bill was next morning pasted on the outside of the gate, offering a reward of five pounds to anybody who would take Oliver Twist off the hands of the parish. In other words, five pounds and Oliver Twist were offered to any man or woman who wanted an apprentice to any trade, business, or calling.

Charles Dickens, *The Adventures of Oliver Twist.* New York: Oxford University Press, n.d.

DOCUMENT 5: THE TRIAL OF A YOUNG THIEF

At the beginning of his writing career (as for much of his life thereafter), Dickens frequently wandered through the streets of London, carefully observing people, scenes, and places, and recording many of these observations in Sketches by Boz, *his first published book. Since he was particularly interested in the legal process as well as in society's treatment of criminals, he took the opportunity to visit the Old Bailey, the central law court of London. In this sketch, Dickens recounts the details of a court session he attended—the trial of a young thief.*

Curiosity has occasionally led us[1] into both Courts at the Old Bailey. Nothing is so likely to strike the person who enters them for the first time, as the calm indifference with which the proceedings are conducted; every trial seems a mere matter of business. There is a great deal of form, but no compassion; considerable interest, but no sympathy. Take the Old Court for example. There sit the Judges, with whose great dignity everybody is acquainted, and of whom therefore we need say no more. Then, there is the Lord Mayor in the centre, looking as cool as a Lord Mayor *can* look, with an immense *bouquet* before him, and habited in all the splendour of his office. Then, there are the Sheriffs, who are almost as dignified as the Lord Mayor himself; and the Barristers, who are quite dignified enough in their own opinion; and the spectators, who having paid for their admission, look upon the whole scene as if it were got up especially for their amusement. Look upon the whole group in the body of the Court—some wholly engrossed in the morning papers, others carelessly conversing in low whispers, and others, again, quietly dozing away an hour—and you can scarcely believe that the result of the trial is a matter of life or death to one wretched being present. But turn your eyes to the dock; watch the prisoner atten-

1. Dickens's sketch is written in first person plural instead of first person singular.

tively for a few moments; and the fact is before you, in all its painful reality. Mark how restlessly he has been engaged for the last ten minutes, in forming all sorts of fantastic figures with the herbs which are strewed upon the ledge before him; observe the ashy paleness of his face when a particular witness appears, and how he changes his position and wipes his clammy forehead and feverish hands, when the case for the prosecution is closed, as if it were a relief to him to feel that the jury knew the worst.

The defence is concluded; the judge proceeds to sum up the evidence; and the prisoner watches the countenances of the jury, as a dying man, clinging to life to the very last, vainly looks in the face of his physician for a slight ray of hope. They turn round to consult; you can almost hear the man's heart beat, as he bites the stalk of rosemary, with a desperate effort to appear composed. They resume their places—a dead silence prevails as the foreman delivers in the verdict—"Guilty!" A shriek bursts from a female in the gallery; the prisoner casts one look at the quarter from whence the noise proceeded; and is immediately hurried from the dock by the gaoler [jailer]. The clerk directs one of the officers of the Court to "take the woman out," and fresh business is proceeded with, as if nothing had occurred.

No imaginary contrast to a case like this, could be as complete as that which is constantly presented in the New Court, the gravity of which is frequently disturbed in no small degree, by the cunning and pertinacity of juvenile offenders. A boy of thirteen is tried, say for picking the pocket of some subject of her Majesty, and the offence is about as clearly proved as an offence can be. He is called upon for his defence, and contents himself with a little declamation about the jurymen and his country—asserts that all the witnesses have committed perjury, and hints that the police force generally have entered into a conspiracy "again" him. However probable this statement may be, it fails to convince the Court, and some such scene as the following then takes place:

Court: Have you any witnesses to speak to your character, boy?

Boy: Yes, my Lord; fifteen gen'lm'n is a vaten [waiting] outside, and vos a vaten all day yesterday, vich [which] they told me the night afore my trial vos a comin' on.

Court: Inquire for these witnesses.

Here, a stout beadle runs out, and vociferates [calls out loudly] for the witnesses at the very top of his voice; for you hear his cry grow fainter and fainter as he descends the steps into the court-yard below. After an absence of five minutes, he returns, very warm and hoarse, and informs the Court of what it knew perfectly well before—namely, that there are no such witnesses in attendance. Hereupon, the boy sets up a most awful howling; screws the lower part of the palms of his hands into the corners of his eyes; and endeavours to look the picture of injured innocence. The jury at once find him "guilty," and his endeavours to squeeze out a tear or two are redoubled. The governor of the gaol [jail] then states, in reply to an inquiry from the bench, that the prisoner has been under his care twice before. This the urchin resolutely denies in some such terms as—"S'elp [So help] me, gen'lm'n, I never vos [was] in trouble afore—indeed, my Lord, I never vos. It's all a howen [owing] to my having a twin brother, vich has wrongfully got into trouble, and vich is so exactly like me, that no vun [one] ever knows the difference atween us."

This representation, like the defence, fails in producing the desired effect, and the boy is sentenced, perhaps, to seven years' transportation [to a penal colony overseas]. Finding it impossible to excite compassion, he gives vent to his feelings in an imprecation [curse] bearing reference to the eyes of "old big vig!" [curled white wig worn by judges] and as he declines to take the trouble of walking from the dock, is forthwith carried out, congratulating himself on having succeeded in giving everybody as much trouble as possible.

Charles Dickens, "Criminal Courts," in *Sketches by Boz: Illustrative of Everyday Life and Everyday People.* New York: Oxford University Press, 1957.

DOCUMENT 6: CRIMINALS IN *OLIVER TWIST*

In "The Author's Introduction to the Third Edition" of Oliver Twist, the reader is afforded access to the mind of the writer, as Dickens justifies his decision to portray so many criminals in the novel. Acknowledging that he has been criticized for doing so (and, it is implied, for thereby condoning crime), Dickens sets out in this introduction to defend himself by explicitly defining his "aim and object" in Oliver Twist. He argues here that although numerous criminals appear throughout the novel, they are all intended by the author to serve a moral purpose: that is, they exemplify the sordid brutality of the criminal world, in all its ugliness, and they attest to the fate that awaits all such criminals—death by hanging.

. . . When I completed [this tale] . . . I fully expected it would be objected to on some very high moral grounds in some very high moral quarters. The result did not fail to prove the justice of my anticipations.

I embrace the present opportunity of saying a few words in explanation of my aim and object in its production. It is in some sort a duty with me to do so, in gratitude to those who sympathized with me and divined my purpose at the time, and who, perhaps, will not be sorry to have their impression confirmed under my own hand.

It is, it seems, a very coarse and shocking circumstance, that some of the characters in these pages are chosen from the most criminal and degraded of London's population; that Sikes is a thief, and Fagin a receiver of stolen goods; that the boys are pick-pockets, and the girl is a prostitute.

I confess I have yet to learn that a lesson of the purest good may not be drawn from the vilest evil. I have always believed this to be a recognized and established truth, laid down by the greatest men the world has ever seen, constantly acted upon by the best and wisest natures, and confirmed by the reason and experience of every thinking mind. I saw no reason, when I wrote this book, why the very dregs of life, so long as their speech did not offend the ear, should not serve the purpose of a moral, at least as well as its froth and cream. Nor did I doubt that there lay festering in Saint Giles's [slums of London] as good materials towards the Truth as any flaunting in Saint James's [fashionable, expensive area of London].

In this spirit, when I wished to show, in little Oliver, the principle of Good surviving through every adverse circumstance, and triumphing at last; and when I considered among what companions I could try him best, having regard to that kind of men into whose hands he would most naturally fall; I bethought myself of those who figure in these volumes. When I came to discuss the subject more maturely with myself, I saw many strong reasons for pursuing the course to which I was inclined. I had read of thieves by scores—seductive fellows (amiable for the most part), faultless in dress, plump in pocket, choice in horseflesh, bold in bearing, fortunate in gallantry, great at a song, a bottle, pack of cards or dice-box, and fit companions for the bravest. But I had never met . . . with the miserable reality. It appeared to me that to draw a knot of such associates in crime as really do exist; to paint them in all their deformity, in all their wretchedness, in all the squalid poverty of their lives; to show them as they really are, for ever skulking uneasily through the dirtiest paths of life, with the great, black, ghastly gallows closing up their prospect, turn them where they may; it appeared to me that to do this, would be to attempt a something which was greatly needed, and which would be a service to society. And therefore I did it, as I best could.

Charles Dickens [Boz, pseud.], "The Author's Introduction to The Third Edition," in *Oliver Twist; Or, The Parish Boy's Progress,* vol. 1. London: Richard Bentley, 1840.

DOCUMENT 7: THE PRISON SHIPS

Some of the most degrading aspects of the English penal system are suggested early in Dickens's novel Great Expectations, *when young Pip, the narrator of the novel, encounters an escaped convict on the moors. Fearful in appearance, the convict is ragged, unkempt, bruised, starving, and wearing an iron manacle on his leg. Although Pip aids the convict, Magwitch, by bringing him food, the prisoner is soon recaptured. In the following dramatic passage, Pip describes how the convict almost chokes on the feelings of rage and despair he attempts to suppress as he is returned to the prison ship from which he escaped. Here, in just a few lines, Dickens powerfully evokes the horror of incarceration aboard the Hulks, the infamous prison ships used to convey criminals to penal colonies overseas.*

The something that I had noticed before, clicked in the man's throat again, and he turned his back. The boat had returned, and his guard were ready, so we followed him to the landing-place made of rough stakes and stones, and saw him put into the boat, which was rowed by a crew of convicts like himself. No one seemed surprised to see him, or interested in seeing him, or glad to see him, or sorry to see him, or spoke a word, except that somebody in the boat growled as if to dogs, 'Give way, you!' which was the signal for the dip of the oars. By the light of the torches, we saw the black Hulk lying out a little way from the mud of the shore, like a wicked Noah's ark. Cribbed and barred and moored by massive rusty chains, the prison-ship seemed in my young eyes to be ironed like the prisoners. We saw the boat go alongside, and we saw him taken up the side and disappear. Then, the ends of the torches were flung hissing into the water, and went out, as if it were all over with him.

Charles Dickens, *Great Expectations*. New York: Oxford University Press, 1953.

DOCUMENT 8: A VISIT TO NEWGATE PRISON

Dickens displayed a lifelong interest in prisons and prison-reform (originating, contend most of his biographers, in his memory of his own father's imprisonment for debt). In this excerpt from one of the most well-known of the Sketches by Boz, *Dickens describes his visit to notorious Newgate prison. Here, the reader is offered a glimpse of some of the most wretched and pitiful of its inhabitants—namely, the female prisoners, old and young, and the boys under fourteen.*

We[1] saw the prison [Newgate], and saw the prisoners; and what we did see, and what we thought, we will tell at once in our own way....

Turning to the right, . . . we came to a door composed of thick bars of wood, through which were discernible, passing to and fro in a narrow yard, some twenty women: the majority of whom, however, as soon as they were aware of the presence of strangers, retreated to their wards. One side of this yard is railed off at a considerable distance, and formed into a kind of iron cage, about five feet ten inches in height, roofed at the top, and defended in front by iron bars, from which the friends of the female prisoners communicate with them. In one corner of this singular-looking den, was a yellow, haggard, decrepit old woman, in a tattered gown that had once been black, and the remains of an old straw bonnet, with faded ribbon of the same hue, in earnest conversation with a young girl—a prisoner, of course—of about two-and-twenty. It is impossible to imagine a more poverty-stricken object, or a creature so borne down in soul and body, by excess of misery and destitution, as the old woman. The girl was a good-looking robust female, with a profusion of hair streaming about in the wind—for she had no bonnet on—and a man's silk pocket-handkerchief loosely thrown over a most ample pair of shoulders. The old woman was talking in

1. Dickens's sketch is written in first person plural instead of first person singular.

that low, stifled tone of voice which tells so forcibly of mental anguish; and every now and then burst into an irrepressible sharp,
abrupt cry of grief, the most distressing sound that ears can hear.
The girl was perfectly unmoved. Hardened beyond all hope of redemption, she listened doggedly to her mother's entreaties, whatever they were: and, beyond inquiring after "Jem," and eagerly
catching at the few halfpence her miserable parent had brought
her, took no more apparent interest in the conversation than the
most unconcerned spectators. Heaven knows there were enough of
them, in the persons of the other prisoners in the yard, who were
no more concerned by what was passing before their eyes, and
within their hearing, than if they were blind and deaf. Why should
they be? Inside the prison, and out, such scenes were too familiar
to them, to excite even a passing thought, unless of ridicule or contempt for feelings which they had long since forgotten.

A little farther on, a squalid-looking woman in a slovenly, thick-
bordered cap, with her arms muffled in a large red shawl, the
fringed ends of which straggled nearly to the bottom of a dirty white
apron, was communicating some instructions to *her* visitor—her
daughter evidently. The girl was thinly clad, and shaking with the
cold. Some ordinary word of recognition passed between her and
her mother when she appeared at the grating, but neither hope,
condolence, regret, nor affection was expressed on either side. The
mother whispered her instructions, and the girl received them with
her pinched-up, half-starved features twisted into an expression of
careful cunning. It was some scheme for the woman's defence that
she was disclosing, perhaps; and a sullen smile came over the girl's
face for an instant, as if she were pleased: not so much at the probability of her mother's liberation, as at the chance of her "getting
off" in spite of her prosecutors. The dialogue was soon concluded;
and with the same careless indifference with which they had approached each other, the mother turned towards the inner end of
the yard, and the girl to the gate at which she had entered.

The girl belonged to a class—unhappily but too extensive—the
very existence of which should make men's hearts bleed. Barely
past her childhood, it required but a glance to discover that she was
one of those children, born and bred in neglect and vice, who have
never known what childhood is: who have never been taught to
love and court a parent's smile, or to dread a parent's frown. The
thousand nameless endearments of childhood, its gaiety and its innocence, are alike unknown to them. They have entered at once
upon the stern realities and miseries of life, and to their better nature it is almost hopeless to appeal in after-times, by any of the references which will awaken, if it be only for a moment, some good
feeling in ordinary bosoms, however corrupt they may have become. Talk to *them* of parental solicitude, the happy days of childhood, and the merry games of infancy! Tell them of hunger and the
streets, beggary and stripes, the gin-shop, the station-house, and

the pawnbroker's, and they will understand you. . . .

Retracing our steps to the dismal passage in which we found ourselves at first (and which, by-the-bye, contains three or four dark
cells for the accommodation of refractory prisoners), we were led
through a narrow yard to the "school"—a portion of the prison set
apart for boys under fourteen years of age. In a tolerable-sized
room, in which were writing-materials and some copy-books, was
the schoolmaster, with a couple of his pupils; the remainder having
been fetched from an adjoining apartment, the whole were drawn
up in line for our inspection. There were fourteen of them in all,
some with shoes, some without; some in pinafores without jackets,
others in jackets without pinafores, and one in scarce anything at
all. The whole number, without an exception we believe, had been
committed for trial on charges of pocket-picking; and fourteen such
terrible little faces we never beheld.—There was not one redeeming
feature among them—not a glance of honesty—not a wink expres-
sive of anything but the gallows and the hulks [prison-ships], in the
whole collection. As to anything like shame or contrition, that was
entirely out of the question. They were evidently quite gratified at
being thought worth the trouble of looking at; their idea appeared to
be, that we had come to see Newgate as a grand affair, and that they
were an indispensable part of the show; and every boy as he "fell in"
to the line, actually seemed as pleased and important as if he had
done something excessively meritorious in getting there at all. We
never looked upon a more disagreeable sight, because we never saw
fourteen such hopeless creatures of neglect, before.

Charles Dickens, "A Visit to Newgate," in *Sketches by Boz: Illustrative of Everyday Life
and Everyday People.* New York: Oxford University Press, 1957.

DOCUMENT 9: A HOME FOR FALLEN WOMEN

*Dickens's active interest in social reform—of schools and prisons, in
particular—eventually took practical form. Working together with
Miss Angela Burdett-Coutts, a wealthy young heiress and philanthropist, who was prepared to finance worthwhile educational projects, Dickens helped to establish a Home for Fallen Women in the
West End of London. The home was planned throughout 1846, and
opened in 1847. Its aim was to rehabilitate these women so that they
could function as useful members of society. In order to accomplish
this, Dickens devoted much time and effort to devising ways of reg-
ulating their conduct: He proposed a system of merit and demerit
marks that he describes in this 1846 letter to Miss Coutts.*

Twenty-Sixth May, 1846

In reference to the Asylum [the Home for Fallen Women established in the West End of London], it . . . would be necessary to limit
the number of inmates, but I would make the reception of them as
easy as possible to themselves. I would put it in the power of any
Governor of a London Prison to send an unhappy creature of this

kind (by her own choice of course) straight from his prison, when her term expired, to the asylum. I would put it in the power of any penitent creature to knock at the door, and say For God's sake, take me in. But I would divide the interior into two portions; and into the first portion I would put all new-comers without exception, as a place of probation, whence they should pass, by their own good conduct and self-denial alone, into what I may call the Society of the house. I do not know of any plan, so well conceived, or so firmly grounded in a knowledge of human nature, or so judiciously addressed to it, for observance in this place, as what is called Captain Maconnochie's Mark System, which I will try very roughly and generally, to describe.

A woman or girl coming to the asylum, it is explained to her that she has come there for *useful* repentance and reform, and means her past way of life has been dreadful in its nature and consequences, and full of affliction, misery, and despair to *herself.* Never mind society while she is at that pass. Society has used her ill and turned away from her, and she cannot be expected to take much heed of its rights or wrongs. It is destructive to herself, and there is no hope in it, or in her, as long as she pursues it. It is explained to her that she is degraded and fallen, but not lost, having this shelter; and that the means of Return to Happiness are now about to be put into her own hands, and trusted to her own keeping. That with this view, she is instead of being placed in this probationary class for a month, or two months, or three months, or any specified *time* whatever, required to earn there a certain number of *Marks* (they are mere scratches in a book) so that she may make her probation a very short one, or a very long one, according to her own conduct. For so much work, she has so many marks; for a day's good conduct, so many more. For every instance of ill-temper, disrespect, bad language, any outbreak of any sort or kind, so many—a very large number in proportion to her receipts—are deducted. A perfect Debtor and Creditor account is kept between her and the Superintendent, for every day; and the state of that account, it is in her own power and nobody else's, to adjust to her advantage. It is expressly pointed out to her, that before she can be considered qualified to return to any kind of society—even to the Society of the asylum—she must give proofs of her power of self-restraint and her sincerity, and her determination to try to shew that she deserves the confidence it is proposed to place in her. Her pride, emulation, her sense of shame, her heart, her reason, and her interest, are all appealed to at once, and if she pass through this trial, she *must* (I believe it to be in the eternal nature of things) rise somewhat in her own self-respect. . . . I would carry a modification of this mark system through the whole establishment; for it is its great philosophy and its chief excellence that it is not a mere form or course of training adapted to the life within the house, but is a preparation—which is a much higher consideration—for the right performance of duty outside, and for the formation of habits of firmness and self-restraint.

Charles Dickens, *The Letters of Charles Dickens, 1832–1846*, vol. 1, ed. Walter Dexter. Bloomsbury, UK: The Nonesuch Press, 1938.

DOCUMENT 10: COKETOWN

Taken from Dickens's novel Hard Times, *this passage depicts the ugliness of Coketown, blighted and polluted as it is by the noxious smoke of coal-burning factories. Such factories flourished in England after the Industrial Revolution took place in the late eighteenth and early nineteenth centuries, enabling manufacturers to produce goods on a large scale. Dickens shows his awareness here that the price paid for such economic progress was the widespread industrial pollution of English towns and cities.*

Coketown . . . was a town of red brick, or of brick that would have been red if the smoke and ashes had allowed it; but as matters stood it was a town of unnatural red and black like the painted face of a savage. It was a town of machinery and tall chimneys, out of which interminable serpents of smoke trailed themselves for ever and ever, and never got uncoiled. It had a black canal in it, and a river that ran purple with ill-smelling dye, and vast piles of building full of windows where there was a rattling and a trembling all day long, and where the piston of the steam-engine worked monotonously up and down like the head of an elephant in a state of melancholy madness. It contained several large streets all very like one another, and many small streets still more like one another, inhabited by people equally like one another, who all went in and out at the same hours, with the same sound upon the same pavements, to do the same work, and to whom every day was the same as yesterday and tomorrow, and every year the counterpart of the last and the next. . . .

Day was shining radiantly upon the town then, and the bells were going for the morning work. Domestic fires were not yet lighted, and the high chimneys had the sky to themselves. Puffing out their poisonous volumes, they would not be long in hiding it; but, for half an hour, some of the many windows were golden, which showed the Coketown people a sun eternally in eclipse, through a medium of smoked glass.

Charles Dickens, *Hard Times.* New York: E.P. Dutton, 1907.

DOCUMENT 11: LONDON FOG

Dickens's novel Bleak House *begins here, with this detailed description of London in winter, with the city enveloped in smoke, soot, and, especially, fog. It soon becomes evident that the fog is intended to be taken both literally and figuratively: It shows the pollution of the city, but it also symbolizes the corruption of the Court of Chancery.*

LONDON. Michaelmas Term lately over, and the Lord Chancellor sitting in Lincoln's Inn Hall [one of London's four law courts]. Implacable November weather. As much mud in the streets, as if the waters had but newly retired from the face of the earth, and it would not be wonderful to meet a Megalosaurus, forty feet long or so, waddling like an elephantine lizard up Holborn Hill. Smoke lowering down from chimney-pots, making a soft, black drizzle, with flakes of soot in it as big as full-grown snowflakes—gone into mourning, one might imagine, for the death of the sun. Dogs, undistinguishable in mire. Horses, scarcely better; splashed to their very blinkers. Foot passengers, jostling one another's umbrellas, in a general infection of ill-temper, and losing their foothold at street corners, where tens of thousands of other foot passengers have been slipping and sliding since the day broke (if the day ever broke), adding new deposits to the crust upon crust of mud, sticking at those points tenaciously to the pavement, and accumulating at compound interest.

Fog everywhere. Fog up the river, where it flows among green aits [little islands] and meadows; fog down the river, where it rolls defiled among the tiers of shipping, and the waterside pollutions of a great (and dirty) city. Fog on the Essex marshes, fog on the Kentish heights. Fog creeping into the cabooses of collier-brigs; fog lying out on the yards, and hovering in the rigging of great ships; fog drooping on the gunwales of barges and small boats. Fog in the eyes and throats of ancient Greenwich pensioners, wheezing by the firesides of their wards; fog in the stem and bowl of the afternoon pipe of the wrathful skipper, down in his close cabin; fog cruelly pinching the toes and fingers of his shivering little 'prentice boy on deck. Chance people on the bridges peeping over the parapets into a nether sky of fog, with fog all round them, as if they were up in a balloon, and hanging in the misty clouds.

Gas looming through the fog in divers places in the streets, much as the sun may, from the spongy fields, be seen to loom by husbandman and ploughboy. Most of the shops lighted two hours before their time—as the gas seems to know, for it has a haggard and unwilling look.

The raw afternoon is rawest, and the dense fog is densest, and the muddy streets are muddiest, near that leaden-headed old obstruction, appropriate ornament for the threshold of a leaden-headed old corporation—Temple Bar. And hard by Temple Bar [another law court], in Lincoln's Inn Hall, at the very heart of the fog, sits the Lord High Chancellor in his High Court of Chancery.

Never can there come fog too thick, never can there come mud and mire too deep, to assort with the groping and floundering condition which this High Court of Chancery, most pestilent of hoary sinners, holds, this day, in the sight of heaven and earth.

Charles Dickens, *Bleak House*. London: Collins, 1953.

DOCUMENT 12: THE MARTYRS OF CHANCERY

*This unsigned article (attributed by some scholars to a journalist, A.
Cole), was published by Dickens in his popular weekly journal,
Household Words, on December 7, 1850, the first of two articles on
the subject. As may be seen in the following excerpt, this is a powerful indictment of the corrupt practices of the Court of Chancery,
which tried people who owed money but were bankrupt. These un-
fortunates, ordered by the Court of Chancery to pay their debts and
to meet their financial obligations, were jailed—often indefinitely—
if they were unable to do so. The growing public criticism of the travesty of justice administered by the Court of Chancery was felt particularly keenly by Dickens because his own father had been
imprisoned for debt in the Marshalsea prison.*

In Lambeth Marsh stands a building better known than honoured.
The wealthy merchant knows it as the place where an unfortunate
friend, who made that ruinous speculation during the recent
sugar-panic, is now a denizen: the man-about-town knows it as a
spot to which several of his friends have been driven, at full gallop,
by fleet race horses and dear dog-carts: the lawyer knows it as the
"last scene of all," the catastrophe of a large proportion of law-suits:
the father knows it as a bugbear wherewith to warn his scapegrace
spendthrift son; but the uncle knows it better as the place whence
nephews date protestations of reform and piteous appeals, "this
once," for bail. Few, indeed, are there who has not heard of the
Queen's Prison, or, as it is more briefly and emphatically termed,
"The Bench."

Awful sound! What visions of folly and roguery, of sloth and
seediness, of ruin and recklessness, are conjured up to the imagination in these two words! It is the "Hades" of commerce—the "Inferno" of fortune. Within its grim walls . . . dwell at this moment
members of almost every class of society. Debt—the grim incubus
riding on the shoulders of his victim, like the hideous old man in
the Eastern fable—has here his captives safely under lock and key,
and within fifty-feet walls. The church, the army, the navy, the bar,
the press, the turf, the trade of England, have each and all their rep-
resentatives in this "house." Every grade, from the ruined man of
fortune to the petty tradesman who has been undone by giving
credit to others still poorer than himself, sends its members to this
Bankrupts' Parliament.

Nineteen-twentieths in this Royal House of Detention owe their
misfortunes directly or indirectly to themselves; and, for them,
every free and prosperous man has his cut and dry moral, or scrap
of pity, or screed of advice; but there is a proportion of prisoners—
happily a small one—within those huge brick boundaries, who
have committed no crime, broken no law, infringed no command-
ment. They are the victims of a system which has been bequeathed
to us from the dark days of the "Star Chambers," and "Courts of

High Commission"—we mean the Martyrs of Chancery.

These unhappy persons were formerly confined in the Fleet Prison, but on the demolition of that edifice, were transferred to the Queen's Bench. Unlike prisoners of any other denomination, they are frequently ignorant of the cause of their imprisonment, and more frequently still, are unable to obtain their liberation by any acts or concessions of their own. There is no act of which they are permitted to take the benefit; no door left open for them in the Court of Bankruptcy. A Chancery prisoner is, in fact, a far more hopeless mortal than a convict sentenced to transportation [to a penal colony]; for the latter knows that, at the expiration of a certain period, he will, in any event, be a free man. The Chancery prisoner has no such certainty; he may, and he frequently does, waste a lifetime in the walls of a gaol [jail], whither he was sent in innocence; because, perchance, he had the ill-luck to be one of the next of kin of some testator who made a will which no one could comprehend, or the heir of some intestate who made none. Any other party interested in the estate commences a Chancery suit, which he must defend or be committed to prison for "contempt." A prison is his portion, whatever he does; for, if he answers the bill filed against him, and cannot pay the costs, he is also clapped in gaol for "contempt." Thus, what in ordinary life is but an irrepressible expression of opinion or a small discourtesy, is, "in Equity," a high crime punishable with imprisonment—sometimes perpetual. Whoever is pronounced guilty of contempt in a Chancery sense is taken from his family, his profession, or his trade (perhaps his sole means of livelihood), and consigned to a gaol where he must starve, or live on a miserable pittance of three shillings and six-pence a week charitably doled out to him from the county rate.

Disobedience of an order of the Court of Chancery—though that order may command you to pay more money than you ever had, or to hand over property which is not yours and was never in your possession—is contempt of court. . . . For this there is no pardon. You are in the catalogue of the doomed, and are doomed accordingly.

A popular fallacy spreads a notion that no one need "go into Chancery" unless he pleases. Nothing but an utter and happy innocence of the bitter irony of "Equity" proceedings keeps such an idea current. Men have been imprisoned for many years, some for a lifetime, on account of Chancery proceedings of the very existence of which they were almost in ignorance before they "somehow or other were found in contempt."

"The Martyrs of Chancery," *Household Words: A Weekly Journal*, vol. 2, September 28, 1850–March 22, 1851.

Chronology

1812

Britain and the United States are at war. Napoléon Bonaparte and his French army retreat from Moscow. Charles Dickens is born on February 7 in Portsmouth, southern England, to John Dickens, a clerk in the Naval Pay Office, and Elizabeth Barrow Dickens.

1815

The Napoleonic Wars end in Europe.

1824

Young Charles is sent to work at Warren's Blacking Factory, and his father is imprisoned for debt in the Marshalsea.

1830

Dickens falls in love with Maria Beadnell. He begins to work as a parliamentary reporter for the *Mirror of Parliament.*

1832

Parliament passes the First Reform Act to change the British electoral system: It extends the franchise, or right to vote, to small-property holders; it also reapportions electoral districts to include industrial towns with large populations instead of only small boroughs, dominated by the nobility and gentry, as previously.

1833–1835

Parliament abolishes slavery throughout the British colonies. Lord Althrop's Factory Act mitigates child labor.

1836

Dickens marries Catherine "Kate" Hogarth. He publishes his first book, *Sketches by Boz,* and becomes involved in theater production. His second book, *Pickwick Papers,* is published serially from March 31, 1836, to November 18, 1837.

1837

Victoria is crowned queen of England. *Oliver Twist* is published serially from February 1837 to April 1839 in *Bentley's Miscellany.*

1838

Nicholas Nickleby is published serially from April 1838 to October 1839.

1839

Chartist riots break out in May when Parliament rejects the Chartist petition for workers' rights and universal male suffrage. Further Chartist riots erupt in November.

1840

Dickens founds *Master Humphrey's Clock*, a weekly magazine in which he serializes *The Old Curiosity Shop* from April 25, 1840, to February 6, 1841.

1841

Barnaby Rudge is serialized in *Master Humphrey's Clock* from February 13, 1841, to November 17, 1841.

1842

Parliament passes Ashley's Act, abolishing female labor in mines. The act also specifies that no boy under ten years of age can work underground. Dickens visits the United States.

1843

Martin Chuzzlewit is published serially from January 1843 to July 1844. *A Christmas Carol* is published on December 19, 1843.

1846

Dombey and Son is published serially from October 1846 to April 1848.

1847

Parliament passes the Ten Hours Act, limiting the working day of women and children in textile factories to ten hours. Dickens helps establish a home in London for impoverished women and prostitutes.

1848

Parliament again rejects a Chartist petition. Revolutions break out in many European countries.

1849

David Copperfield is published serially from May 1849 to November 1850.

1850

Parliament passes the Factory Act, establishing a ten-and-a-half-hour workday. Dickens establishes and edits *Household Words*, a weekly journal.

1852

Bleak House is published serially from March 1852 to September 1853.

1853

Dickens gives the first of his public readings in England.

1854

The Crimean War begins and continues until 1856. *Hard Times* is serialized weekly in *Household Words* from April 1 to August 12, 1854.

1855

Little Dorrit is published serially from December 1855 to June 1857.

1858

Dickens begins his notorious affair with married actress Ellen Ternan. He announces his separation from his wife, Catherine.

1859

Dickens founds and edits a new weekly journal, *All the Year Round*, in which *A Tale of Two Cities* is published serially from April 20 to November 26, 1859.

1860

Great Expectations is serialized weekly in *All the Year Round* from December 1, 1860, to August 3, 1861.

1861–1865

The American Civil War is fought.

1862

Abraham Lincoln issues the Emancipation Proclamation, freeing slaves in the seceding states.

1864

Our Mutual Friend is published serially from May 1864 to November 1865.

1867

Parliament passes the Second Reform Act to further democratize the British electoral system. It extends voting rights to various working men in towns and cities. It is followed some years later by the Third Reform Act of 1884–1885, which extends the vote to agricultural workers. The number of (male) voters is thereby greatly increased. Dickens visits America again, this time on a reading tour.

1869

Parliament abolishes imprisonment for debt.

1870

The serialization of Dickens's last novel, *The Mystery of Edwin Drood*, commences in April 1870, but the work is never completed. Charles Dickens dies of a cerebral hemorrhage on June 9, 1870, and is buried in Westminster Abbey.

FOR FURTHER RESEARCH

NOVELS BY DICKENS

Charles Dickens, *Bleak House*. New York: Penguin Putnam, 1994.

———, *David Copperfield*. New York: Penguin Putnam, 1994.

———, *Great Expectations*. New York: Penguin Putnam, 1994.

———, *Hard Times*. New York: Penguin Putnam, 1994.

———, *Oliver Twist*. New York: Penguin Putnam, 1994.

———, *A Tale of Two Cities*. New York: Penguin Putnam, 1994.

Editor's note: Penguin is but one of several editions of Dickens's novels; others are Norton Critical Editions, Riverside World's Classics, and Signet.

VICTORIAN CULTURE AND THOUGHT

Barbara Dennis and David Skilton, *Reform and Intellectual Debate in Victorian England*. New York: Croom Helm, 1987.

J.M. Golby, ed., *Culture and Society in Britain, 1850–1890: A Source Book of Contemporary Writings*. Oxford, UK: Oxford University Press, 1986.

T.W. Heyck, *The Transformation of Intellectual Life in Victorian England*. Ed. Richard Price. London: Croom Helm, 1982.

Walter E. Houghton, *The Victorian Frame of Mind, 1830–1870*. New Haven, CT: Yale University Press, 1975.

Alice Jenkins and Juliet John, eds., *Rereading Victorian Fiction*. New York: St. Martin's, 2000.

Gordon Marsden, ed., *Victorian Values: Personalities and Per-*

spectives in Nineteenth Century Society. New York: Longman, 1990.

Eric M. Sigsworth, ed., *In Search of Victorian Values: Aspects of Nineteenth Century Thought and Society.* Manchester, UK: Manchester University Press, 1988.

Geoffrey Tillotson, *A View of Victorian Literature.* Oxford, UK: Clarendon Press, 1978.

BIOGRAPHIES OF DICKENS

Ivor Brown, *Dickens in His Time.* London: Thomas Nelson, 1963.

Martin Fido, *Charles Dickens.* London: Hamlyn, 1985.

John Forster, *The Life of Charles Dickens.* 2 vols. New York: Dutton, 1980.

Edgar Johnson, *Charles Dickens: His Tragedy and Triumph.* 2 vols. London: Victor Gollancz, 1953.

Fred Kaplan, *Dickens: A Biography.* London: Hodder and Stoughton, 1988.

Norman and Jeanne MacKenzie, *Dickens: A Life.* New York: Oxford University Press, 1979.

Alan S. Watts, *The Life and Times of Charles Dickens.* London: Studio Editions, 1991.

Angus Wilson, *The World of Charles Dickens.* London: Martin Secker and Warburg, 1970.

STUDIES OF DICKENS'S WORKS

Ron Abbott and Charlie Bell, *Charles Dickens: A Beginner's Guide.* Abingdon, UK: Hodder and Stoughton, 2001.

Peter Ackroyd, *Introduction to Dickens.* London: Mandarin, 1991.

Harold Bloom, ed., *Charles Dickens.* Broomall, PA: Main Line Book, 2000.

Frank Donovan, *The Children of Charles Dickens.* London: Leslie Frewin, 1969.

Allan Grant, *A Preface to Dickens.* New York: Longman, 1984.

Barbara Hardy, *Charles Dickens: The Writer and His Work.* Windsor, UK: Profile Books, 1983.

Philip Hobsbaum, *A Reader's Guide to Charles Dickens*. London: Thames and Hudson, 1972.

F.R. Leavis and Q.D. Leavis, *Dickens the Novelist*. London: Chatto and Windus, 1970.

Robert B. Partlow Jr., ed., *Dickens the Craftsman: Strategies of Presentation*. Carbondale: Southern Illinois University Press, 1970.

Martin Price, ed., *Dickens: A Collection of Critical Essays*. Englewood Cliffs, NJ: Prentice-Hall, 1967.

E.W.F. Tomlin, ed., *Charles Dickens, 1812–1870: A Centenary Volume*. London: Weidenfeld and Nicolson, 1969.

Edmund Wilson, "The Two Scrooges," in *The Wound and The Bow: Seven Studies in Literature*. Rev. ed. London: W.H. Allen, 1952.

DICKENS WEBSITES

The Charles Dickens Page, www.fidnet.com/~dap1955/ dickens. This website, run by David Perdue, has a wealth of resources. It has an alphabetical listing of the characters in Dickens's novels as well as summaries of the novels. It provides information on Dickens's life, including his journalistic career, his trip to America and his influence on Christmas tradition. There is a description and map of London in Dickens's time and a message board where one can post questions.

Dickens House Museum, www.dickensmuseum.com. This website provides a virtual tour of Dickens's one-time residence in London. Although Dickens only lived in this three-story house from 1837 to 1839, it was there that he wrote several of his most famous works, including *Oliver Twist* and *Nicholas Nickleby*. The museum, which opened in 1925, is dedicated to the life and work of Dickens, and the interior of the house has been restored in the style of the Victorian era. After touring the house, one can connect to other websites about Dickens and his work.

The Dickens Information Page, http://lang.nagoya-u.ac.ip/~ matsuoka/Dickens.html. This enormous website, run by Mitsuharo Matsuoka, contains an extensive network of resources. On the website itself is a chronology of Dickens's life, a family tree, mailing lists, and information on scholarly conferences and publications. In addition, for each of Dickens's works, there are several dozen links to websites on that particular work, to articles about the novel, and to discussion boards and other relevant information for that work.

The Dickens Project, http://humwww.ucsc.edu/dickens. This excellent website is run by the Dickens Project, a consortium of U.S. and international universities based at the University of California at Santa Cruz, which was established in 1981 to disseminate research on Charles Dickens and his time. The website lists details of the project's publications, the annual conferences held at Santa Cruz, readers' theater scripts, and even information on a fellowship for students interested in studying Dickens further. The site also contains an electronic archive on Dickens, biographical information, and links to related sites.

Victoria Research Web, www/indiana.edu/~victoria. This website has been assembled by the creator and manager of the VICTORIA discussion list, a listserv for scholars and researchers interested in the Victorian era. The site has extensive bibliographies and an archive with information on such diverse subjects as nineteenth-century census data and publishers' records, as well as more mainstream research information. The site also has a section on practical matters, such as places to stay in London and Victorian places of interest to visit there.

INDEX